COUNTRY MUSIC

CHARTWELL
BOOKS INC.

in association with Phoebus

Written by
Bryan Chalker
with additional material by
Mick Houghton, Chris Salewicz
and Dick Tatham

Edited by Jeremy Pascall
Designed by Rob Burt

Unless otherwise specified, pictures by courtesy
of the Chalker Collection and recording companies.

Published by Chartwell Books Inc.
A Division of Book Sales Inc.
110 Enterprise Avenue
Secaucus, New Jersey 07094

Library of Congress Catalog
Card Number 76-14642

© 1976 Phoebus Publishing Company
BPC Publishing Limited
169 Wardour Street
LONDON W1A 2JX

ISBN 0 7026 0015 6

Filmsetting and Reproduction by
Petty & Sons Ltd., Leeds.
Made and printed in Great Britain by
Waterlow (Dunstable) Limited

CONTENTS

THIS IS...
COUNTRY MUSIC

Country music has been aptly described as the music of the people, for the people, by the people. Its vast appeal lies in its direct simplicity; its ability to get straight to the heart. Basic country music is easy to perform and audiences have always been able to identify with the sentiments expressed in the majority of country songs. Today country covers a whole range of music from styles as dissimilar as Cajun and Rockabilly and artists as diverse as Tammy Wynette and Emmylou Harris, Roger Miller and Kris Kristofferson, Marty Robbins and the Nitty Gritty Dirt Band. And it covers a musical heritage that includes names as lustrous as Hank Williams, Roy Acuff, Carson J. Robison and the Carter Family. All come under the broad canopy of country music.

Universal Appeal

What is it about country that unites and delights millions of people all over the world? Perhaps part of the appeal of country songs is that they often deal with universal subjects — love, romance, heartbreak — and tell truths about them that strike a sympathetic chord in the listener. Frequently, of course, the songs tell a story, a story about ordinary people. Carson J. Robison, a prolific and highly successful singer-songwriter of the '30s and '40s explained the immense popularity of the sort of ballads he wrote in this way: 'There's a formula, of course. You start by painting everything in gay colours – 'the folks were happy and gay' stuff. That's surefire. Then you ring in the tragedy — make it as morbid and gruesome as you can. Then you wind up with a moral.'' Although he was describing the process with his tongue firmly in cheek, there's some basic truth in the description.

The term Country music, or Country and Western, as it was once called, is a generalization for a multitude of sounds and styles that include Folk, Old-Time, Gospel, Bluegrass, Western-Swing, Rock-

Sound. These in turn may be sub-divided into subject-matter classifications such as: Honky-Tonk, Railroad, Truckers, Cowboys, Traditional and Heart. With the possible exception of honky-tonk and heart songs, the remainder are self-explanatory. Honky-tonk songs were the sleazy, working-class bar-room juke-box favourites of the '40s and '50s popularized by artists like Ernest Tubb & His Texas Troubadours, Lefty Frizzell, Hank Thompson, Kitty Wells and Charley Walker, whereas 'heart' songs or 'weepers' as early country magazines were wont to call them, formed the foundations for today's sentimental but more sophisticated commercial country ballads.

Country is the musical soul of white America laid bare. It draws its roots from the folk heritage of the British Isles, from German lieder and French peasant dances and a multitude of other sources. Country, claimed one American journalist, is the oldest *new* music in a thousand years. Commercialization has overtaken it to a large extent but the old folk legends like John Henry, Barbara Allen and The Knoxville Tragedy are still recalled from time to time and the reels, jigs and hornpipes remain an integral part of those styles of country known as Bluegrass and Old-Time.

Respected Heritage

Bluegrass is confined, by tradition, to five unamplified stringed instruments, guitar, mandolin, fiddle, string-bass and banjo. The five-string banjo, played in the three-finger style (as developed by Snuffy Jenkins, Smith Hammed, Fischer Hendley and popularized by Earl Scruggs in 1945) provides Bluegrass with its characteristic sound. Old-Time music, on the other hand, adheres less rigidly to these instrumental limitations and whilst the fiddle, string bass, guitar, mandolin and banjo form the basis of many Old-Time bands, they are often augmented by autoharp, Appalachian dulcimer, dobro guitar, snaredrum and harmonica. The majority of Old-Time bands

hammer' style of banjo playing, which is far more fluid than Scruggs's three-finger method.

The years since the '60s have seen a progression from the old three-chord

works calling for sophisticated arrangements and interpretations. Writers like Kris Kristofferson, Mac Davis, Mickey Newbury and Willie Nelson have added new dimensions to the folk music of America; but they still draw their inspirations from life.

Ironically the cowboy, possibly the greatest of all-American folk heroes, figures sparsely in the overall concept of country music. His songs and ballads have now been relegated to the realms of traditional 'folk' music and the truck driver and railroad engineer have taken his place as the contemporary heroes and symbols of freedom. He still has his place, however, in this most varied of music forms. All of this then is country music . . .

Bluegrass Music

To say that America has no indigenous music is a misnomer for, amid the German lieder, Scottish rants, reels and strathspeys, Irish jigs and hornpipes, sedate quadrilles and quaint medieval English ballads that make up the grass roots of the United States' folk music culture, there evolved a hybrid known latterly as bluegrass.

The development of bluegrass took place over three centuries and was the result of a fusion of musical elements and cultural exchanges, a blending of fiddle and banjo styles, climaxed by the creative genius of a Kentucky-born musician called Bill Monroe.

It would be inaccurate to say that bluegrass music in its modern form is an essentially historical sound, because the characteristic three-finger, five-string banjo style that identifies it from other forms of rural American music was not introduced professionally until 1945. Hitherto the banjo style usually adopted by string bands had been the frailing or 'clawhammer' method, in which the strings are struck in a downwards motion. Nevertheless, in the mid-'70s bluegrass purported to be the traditional music indigenous to the Americas.

In its basic workings bluegrass can be compared to Dixieland Jazz; both are 'assembly forms', in that each instrument, be it fiddle, clarinet, banjo or trombone, has a specific role to fulfil within the band's structure and one that is strictly adhered to.

String band music, which reached its zenith in the '20s and '30s, developed out of a need for simple musical recreation during America's pioneer period. Many of the early musicians drew heavily from the Negro blues repertoire, as well as from white traditional musical styles and by the end of the '30s the foundations for modern bluegrass had been laid.

Countless rural string bands contributed to the ultimate creation of bluegrass and among the more notable performers of the period were Uncle Eck Robertson (a fiddle player who influenced many later musicians), J. P. Nester and Norman Edmonds (a banjo-fiddle duo from Virginia), Bill Helms and His Upson County Band, Raymond D. Hundley (a banjo player with the Virginia String Band), Doc Walsh (one of the finest banjo pickers from that era), Pope's Arkansas Mountaineers, the Blue Sky Boys (two brothers, Bill and Earl Bolick, from North Carolina, whose impeccable vocal harmonies inspired numerous bluegrass singers), Charlie Poole and the North Carolina Ramblers, Gid Tanner & the Skillet Lickers, Wade Mainer and Zeke Morris, Roy Hall and his Blue Ridge Entertainers and the Monroe Brothers, Charlie and Bill.

The Monroe Brothers, who began playing and singing professionally in 1934, became one of the most important of these early string bands and their impact on modern country music was tremendous. Bill played mandolin, while Charlie provided a mellow guitar accompaniment and the group's vocal duets — including 'All The Good Times Are Past And Gone' and 'New River Train' — for RCA's Bluebird label and RCA Victor itself, became classics of the genre.

Multitude Of Influences

In 1938, the two brothers decided to pursue individual musical careers and almost immediately Bill formed a group called the Kentuckians, playing out of Little Rock, Arkansas. This particular group was short-lived and after less than three months Monroe had organized a second band, the Blue Grass Boys, comprising mandolin, fiddle, guitar and jug.

Prior to the advent of the three-finger banjo style of 1945, the instrumental structure of string bands was fairly flexible and often included ukulele, autoharp, mandolin, banjo and harmonica. Bill Monroe, however, began to bring a measure of discipline to the music and it wasn't long after he joined the *Grand Ole Opry* show in 1939 that the strict format of bluegrass began to establish itself.

Bill Monroe and the Blue Grass Boys became instant favourites on the *Opry* but it wasn't until 1946 when Monroe's first hit recordings 'Footprints In The Snow' and 'Kentucky Waltz' appeared that the group began to make an impact on a national level.

By the end of World War Two hillbilly bands reflected a multitude of influences. Fiddlers' conventions, rural tent shows, river-boats, home social dances and even churches had provided the ingredients for a wide range of instrumental and vocal styles. Feedback of popular styles — ragtime, urban blues, vaudeville and jazz — into the rural southern areas added to the

Above: The Foggy Mountain Boys band.

diversity of musical elements known to the hillbilly musician by 1945.

Monroe's earlier bands had included accordion in the line-up and whilst many of his musical innovations were coming to the fore, there was none of the complex instrumental interplay for which bluegrass is noted.

Following the success of 'Kentucky Waltz' and 'Footprints In The Snow', Monroe was in constant demand. The Blue Grass Boys travelled extensively and Monroe's technique of presenting shows added to his popularity; he carried a large circus tent, which was erected in small towns and drew tremendous crowds.

Throughout his professional career Monroe employed an incredible array of musicians in his band including, among other luminaries, Lester Flatt and Earl Scruggs. It was Earl Scruggs who, in 1945, introduced his revolutionary three-finger style of banjo playing to the audience of the *Grand Ole Opry*.

Earl was a member of Bill Monroe's Blue Grass Boys at the time and, although it was generally recognized that Scruggs did not invent the style, it was he who developed it into a workable component of

Right: Lester Flatt (top) and Earl Scruggs.

bluegrass music. Other earlier players who favoured the three-finger style were Snuffy Jenkins, Smith Hammed and Fischer Hendley, although theirs was a somewhat ragged and heavy sound compared to the smooth, easy-going Scruggs technique.

According to Scruggs, the banjo had its origins in Arabia thousands of years ago; it consisted of a skin 'head' stretched over a hollow body and strung with three strings. This instrument was carried to the East with the spread of Islam. Negro slaves brought it to the United States from Africa.

Banjo Cult

Other instruments similar to the banjo have existed in India (the ravenastron) and Egypt, (where it was known as a banit). The true American banjo was invented by Joel Sweeney, a native of Appomattox, Virginia, in 1830. Sweeney made a revolutionary modification by adding a fifth string, higher in pitch and next to the lowest pitched string and secured by a peg halfway up the neck.

This new instrument became extremely popular throughout the United States,

Above: Faye Dunaway and Warren Beatty as Bonnie and Clyde in the movie of the same name, which featured the Flatt/Scruggs hit song 'Foggy Mountain Breakdown'.

7

Left: Bill and Earl Bolick, the Blue Sky Boys. Right: Bill Monroe ('Father of Bluegrass') and Ralph Stanley, also of bluegrass fame.

where it held a place in the affections of ordinary people throughout the nineteenth century. At the turn of the twentieth century a decline set in; Sweeney's fifth string was gradually eliminated, the neck was shortened and the head enlarged. This modified instrument became known as the 'tenor' banjo and was a popular feature of jazz bands. Even the popularity of the tenor-banjo waned and by the end of the '30s, no banjos at all were being manufactured in America.

Scruggs and the Blue Grass Boys revived the banjo on the *Opry* in 1945 and a massive banjo-bluegrass cult ensued. Monroe was in the van and he produced an impressive number of hits, among them being 'Blue Moon Of Kentucky', 'Muleskinner Blues', 'Uncle Pen', 'Molly And Ten Brooks' and 'Cryin' Holy Unto The Lord'.

In 1948 Earl Scruggs left the Blue Grass Boys, followed a month later by Lester Flatt, guitarist with the group. Within a matter of weeks Flatt and Scruggs had combined forces to form their own band, the Foggy Mountain Boys.

During the era of rock & roll, bluegrass music was almost annihilated and only Monroe and a few lesser known contemporaries kept to the straight-and-narrow path of 'traditional' unamplified bluegrass. Other groups were forced to sell out to the new musical trend and most fell by the wayside, never to fully re-emerge. Monroe, however, believed in his music and, except for one brief episode when he was persuaded to feature an electric guitar on a recording session, he adhered to his own stringent rules.

The true bluegrass instrumental lineup, as decreed by Monroe, consists of guitar, mandolin, string bass, fiddle and five-string banjo. Apart from the characteristic banjo sound, two other factors set bluegrass aside from other forms of country music; the high-pitched tenor singing as exemplified by Bill Monroe, and the Negro-influenced, bluesy fiddle, identified by its 'slides' and Southern 'chops', as opposed to the more classical bow strokes of the British derivation.

Monroe is the acknowledged 'Father of Bluegrass Music' but numerous others contributed greatly to the ultimate national acceptance of the genre. Possibly the most important of these were the Stanley Brothers and the Clinch Mountain Boys who, at one time, recorded for Columbia during the same period that Bill Monroe was with the label.

New Generation

The Stanley Brothers, Ralph and Carter, were responsible for some of the most beautiful bluegrass vocal harmonies ever recorded and their version of Monroe's classic 'Molly And Ten Brooks' marked the transition from the sound laid down on Monroe's recording of the song, to the actual style of music known as bluegrass. The year was 1948 and the Stanley Brothers vied for popularity with Monroe and his group and Flatt and Scruggs. Some of the most famous songs recorded by Ralph and Carter Stanley and the Clinch Mountain Boys included 'White Dove', 'Gathering Flowers', 'How Far To Little Rock', 'Train 45', 'She's More To Be Pitied', 'No School Bus In Heaven' and 'How Mountain Girls Can Love'.

From a purely commercial aspect, the most successful bluegrass band was that fronted by Lester Flatt and Earl Scruggs and they actually enjoyed pop chart hits with 'The Ballad Of Jed Clampett', 'Petticoat Junction' and 'Foggy Mountain Breakdown' from the movie *Bonnie And Clyde*. Purists, however, are reluctant to accept the music of Flatt and Scruggs on the basis that their band featured such non-bluegrass instruments as drums, harmonica and Dobro guitar. Whilst the Dobro was later absorbed into the bluegrass structure, Monroe himself kept to his own beliefs.

The Dobro came into being in 1928, when the Dopera Brothers, of California, realised the need for additional amplification to the popular Hawaiian guitar. The Dobro's main feature is a convex and concave diaphragm, supporting a spider-web bridge. The bridge and diaphragm are covered by a metal resonator and the distinctive 'whining' notes are produced by means of a steel bar or slide, as opposed to the normal methods of chording. The action is also greatly exaggerated.

In the mid-'70s country-rock groups like Country Gazette popularized bluegrass music — albeit with modern amplification — for a whole new generation, and its influence was never far away from the country-rock scene at large. Jerry Garcia of Grateful Dead fame and Vassar Clements produced a new bluegrass album, 'Old And In The Way' (1975).

Earl Scruggs himself penned what is perhaps the most graphic description of the inspiration for bluegrass music: "Americana. Life yesterday, today and tomorrow. Purest of what this earth has to offer and unaffected by the passing of time. Earthy and spontaneous, uncomplicated, and rooted in the US folk music tradition."

8

Cowboy & Western Music

Above: Gene Autry proved as popular on record as in his 100 movies and 95 TV films.

To the majority of people outside the country music field, the term 'country & western music' is synonymous with covered wagons, rolling Texas plains, sagebrush and grizzled cowpokes herding longhorn steers under a blazing sun. A completely false image, in fact, projected by two distinct styles of music — western swing and the songs and ballads of the Hollywood screen cowboys.

The term 'western' (as applied to country & western) was the title given to a style of dance music popular throughout the south-western states during the '30s and '40s, and performed by such artists as Bob Wills, Leon Selph and Pee Wee King. The late 1920's and early 1930's were experimental years in the field of country music (or hillbilly as it was then known) and while Charlie Poole and the North Carolina Ramblers, the Leake County Revellers, Gid Tanner and the Skillet Lickers, Ernest V. Stoneman and other similar artists were busily recording the more traditional sounds and songs — 'Mountain Reel', 'Fiddlers' Convention In Georgia', 'Ragtime Annie' and 'Goin' Down The Valley', among others — a number of musicians, especially in the south-western states, were introducing a noticeable 'swing' to their material.

Dixie Influence

Although ostensibly a 'country' form, western swing, as this new music came to be known, drew heavily on the field of Dixieland jazz for its inspiration and it was not unusual for early swing bands to record

numbers like the great 'Basin Street Blues'.

Prior to the full emergence of true western swing, countless south-western string bands were playing up-tempo versions of traditional tunes, mixed with variants of standard pop songs, and they were mostly in demand for square dances and the like.

The real innovator of western swing, however, was Bob Wills, who formed his first true swing band in 1931. Wills had

originally worked in a duo called simply Wills Fiddle Band with himself on fiddle and Herman Arnspiger on guitar. Vocalist Milton Brown joined them in 1931 and the name was changed to the Alladin Laddies. In the same year the Light Crust Flour Company became the sponsor for Wills's band on a Fort Worth, Texas, radio station and he was obliged to change the group's name once again — this time Wills chose the title the Light Crust Dough Boys, and they subsequently recorded several moderately successful titles for RCA Victor.

By 1932 Wills had added to the line-up of his band and implemented yet another name change, calling it the Texas Playboys, later to become one of the most revered of all western swing bands. While Wills was an innovator and introduced drums, saxophone, trumpets and numerous fiddles into the band's line-up, he remained relatively faithful to the 'traditional' western swing style and didn't veer too far away from the established country music repertoire of the day.

Western Swing

Milton Brown left the band in 1932 and formed his own swing band, the Musical Brownies, but unlike Wills, Brown's music became more jazz-orientated and ultimately they were little more than a 'westernized' Dixieland jazz band.

Throughout the '30s and '40s the Texas Playboys reigned supreme in the field of western swing, recording such classics as 'San Antonio Rose', 'Texas Playboy', 'Back Home Again In Indiana', 'I Don't Love Nobody', 'Steel Guitar Rag' (which featured the steel playing of Leon McAuliffe) and 'Take Me Back To Tulsa'.

Western swing remained in vogue until the mid-1950's, when it was superseded by a new style which embraced three closely-related facets of country music — honky tonk, rockabilly and the bare remnants of swing. One of the finest exponents of this new style was Buck Owens, until he eventually rang the changes and developed a more commercial pop-influenced sound.

With the exception of certain traditional melodies, the music of the western swing bands was far removed from that of the cowboy. The mode of stage dress adopted by many of the bands — high-heeled Spanish leather boots, ornate, rhinestone-studded jackets, elaborate kerchiefs and Stetsons — undoubtedly gave credence to the 'cowboys and country music' misnomer. In spite of these 'westernized' costumes, however, it was the advent of the singing cowboy during the same period which gave rise to the almost worldwide belief that country music symbolized the Wild West.

The singing cowboy was a Hollywood brainchild and among the first to ride a bronco across the silver screen was John Wayne. Wayne made little impact with his singing and it was left to Gene Autry, a former cattle drover and railroad telegraph operator, to ride to fame.

Autry made his recording debut in 1929, appearing on a variety of labels including Van Dyke and Radiex. In common with many other performers of the time Autry adopted a series of pseudonyms, among them Sam Hill and John Hardy. During the early years of his recording career Autry modelled his style on that of Jimmie Rodgers and on one song in particular, 'In The Jailhouse Now', the vocal resemblance to Rodgers was uncanny.

In 1931, Autry signed a contract with RCA Victor and recorded what many historians consider to be his finest material. Autry's many hits included 'Silver Haired Daddy Of Mine', 'Mexicali Rose', 'Be Honest With Me', 'Tumbling Tumbleweeds', 'You Are My Sunshine', 'Have I Told You Lately That I Love You', 'Rudolph The Red-Nosed Reindeer' and 'Goodbye Little Darling'.

Autry's movie career began in 1935 and he eventually appeared in 100 movies, including *Old Santa Fe* (1935), *Tumbling Tumbleweeds* (1935), *Shooting High* (1940) and *Robin Hood Of Texas* (1947). In addition Autry appeared in 95 half-hour television movies. Autry frequently played the role of an almost clinical, untarnished cowboy, who abhorred unnecessary violence. So wholesome were Autry's movie roles that he was honoured with an award from the National Parent/Teachers Film Association.

Autry set the trend for a whole spate of singing screen cowboys and those who made substantial impacts during the heyday of those trite but wholly enjoyable Westerns were Roy Rogers, Tex Ritter and Rex Allen.

Ritter, later to be affectionately known as 'America's Most Beloved Cowboy', carved his own niche in cinema history by appearing in a total of 68 musical westerns for companies like Monogram, Universal and Columbia. He also portrayed the Lone Ranger in a long-running series. Tex was a vastly different commodity to Autry, insofar as he recorded many traditional western ballads during his career and was an acknowledged authority on cowboy folklore.

Outlaw Myth

The 1950s saw the virtual demise of the musical western but by that time the idea that each and every country singer rode a horse and chased outlaws across the length and breadth of the Lone Star State had been firmly implanted in the public's mind.

Ironically, the authentic music of the true Texas cowboy played a relatively small part in the ultimate development of modern country music. Most cowboy songs were either based on traditional British melodies (i.e., 'The Unfortunate Rake' or 'The Sailor Cut Down In His Prime', which later saw service as 'The Streets Of Laredo') or taken from poems chronicling the west of the last century. Original cowboy melodies were rare and most ballads were sung to a standard selection of no more than five different tunes. Lyrics were passed on by word of mouth from one camp to another and became 'traditional' almost overnight.

Some of the early cowboy songs that have remained virtually intact include 'The Chisholm Trail' (countless variants exist), 'I Ride An Old Paint', 'Brown-Eyed Lee', 'The Buffalo Skinners', 'Zebra Dun', 'Home On The Range', 'I'm Bound To Follow The Longhorn Cow', 'Git Along Little Dogies', 'Little Joe', 'The Wrangler', 'On The Lake Of The Poncho Plains', 'Night Herding Song', 'The Cowboy's Lament' and 'Utah Carroll'.

Above: Movie/cowboy star Tex Ritter.

Above: Harry 'Mac' McClintock.

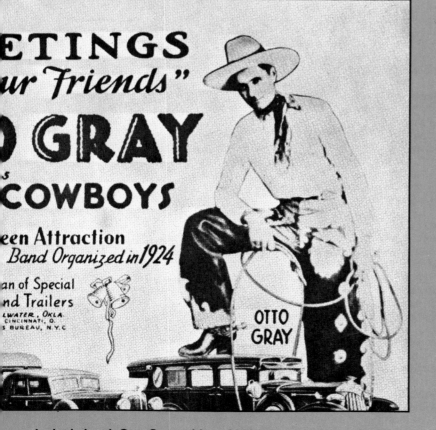

Lariat in hand, Otto Gray, without his famous Oklahoma Cowboys.

In the 1920's various recording companies realized that a market existed for cowboy songs and a number of performers came briefly to the fore. One of the best-known of these artists was an ex-ranch-hand called Carl T. Sprague, who recorded over 30 songs between 1925 and 1934, including 'When The Work's All Done This Fall' (recorded in 1925 and subsequently selling 900,000 copies), 'The Mormon Cowboy' and 'Utah Carroll' among other song hits.

'Zebra Dun'

Almost as popular as Sprague was Jules Verne Allen, a cattle driver from Waxahachie, Texas. Known from time to time as Longhorn Luke, Allen recorded, among others, 'Zebra Dun', 'The Days Of Forty-Nine' and 'The Cowboy's Dream', which became classics.

One of the most popular ballads among the cowboy fraternity was 'The Chisholm Trail', the definitive version of which was recorded in 1928, by another authentic westerner, Haywire Mac, otherwise known as Harry 'Mac' McClintock. Born in Tennessee, in 1882, McClintock became popular through his recordings of traditional cowboy songs and hobo ballads, the best known being 'Cowboy's Lament', 'Hallelujah, I'm A Bum', 'Big Rock Candy Mountains', 'Texas Rangers' and 'Sam Bass' — all great songs in the best cowboy tradition.

Another important traditional performer of the period was Goebel Reeves, the Texas Drifter, who contributed such items as 'Little Joe', 'The Wrangler' and 'Bar None Ranch' to the repertoire of recorded western music. Like others of his ilk, Reeves recorded for a variety of labels using several pseudonyms, among the latter being George Riley, the Broadway Wrangler, Bert Knowles and the Yodelling Rustler.

Contrary to popular belief, the guitar was not liked by the men who worked the cattle ranges; they preferred to sing their ballads unaccompanied and it was only the likes of Carl T. Sprague, Jules Allen, Harry 'Mac' McClintock and Goebel Reeves who introduced a limited amount of instrumentation to the music of the American cowboy.

Authentic performers inspired a host of imitators, most of whom preferred non-traditional material. Most of these pseudo-cowboy artists, whose numbers included such colourful names as Arizona Red, the Lone Star Ranger, Tiny Dodson and his Circle B Boys, Denver Darling, Big Slim (The Lone Cowboy) and Red River Dave McEnery, enjoyed a brief spate of popularity and then drifted once more into obscurity. A few, like Montana Slim (Wilf Carter) and Stuart Hamblen, made sufficient impact on the record-buying public to endure for many years but, in the main, the era of the genuine singing cowboy and his multitudinous host of imitators was short-lived and contributed precious little to the structure of contemporary country music.

Cajun: The French Connection

The people of Louisiana call it "French music," but most devotees outside of the bayou country know it as Cajun (Kay-jun), the traditional music of the Acadians, who originally journeyed to Canada from Normandy, Picardy and Brittany.

When the British and their Indian allies finally defeated the French in the Anglo-French Indian Wars of 1740–63, the people of the province of l'Acadie (later to be called Nova Scotia – New Scotland) were purged by the victorious British forces. The Acadians, claimed British officials, would not swear allegiance to Queen Anne, so they were driven from their homes. In the summer of 1755, during the reign of George II, the British herded 10,000 French settlers aboard 22 tiny ships and transported them from l'Acadie to the southern states of America where countless numbers were sold into slavery; those who escaped settled in French Louisiana. Seven years later Louisiana ceded to Spanish rule but the Acadians were left undisturbed, and in 1803, when the American president, Thomas Jefferson, purchased Louisiana, he, too, left the French in comparative peace.

Soaking Up The Influences

Cajun music was originally the folk balladry of 17th and 18th century France but over the years it had steadily absorbed the fundamental elements of jazz, blues, white country and German music. The most noticeable changes had taken place over the last half-century, with the advent of the gramophone record.

The late Mike Leadbitter, writing in *Country Music Review* (September, 1972), said of the Acadians and their music: "Acadians may have been slow to change their way of life, but have always been quick to draw on the popular sounds around them, being very conscious of the non-Cajun entertainers who've entered French homes or bars via the record player, radio, television and jukebox. A real French musician will thus present a very varied programme but, somehow, always retains his own identity, playing in a unique manner (for it has never been successfully copied) and singing in the local patois wherever he finds it possible."

"The fact that Cajun songs are generally sung in French had led to an almost total ignorance about them and their origins, for few outsiders attempt to appreciate something outside their understanding. The pride, however, that Acadians have in their own music and for its interpreters has always meant that a strong market for authentic Cajun recordings exists and many have catered for an ever-increasing demand over the years, in spite of what others regard as a minority market."

Traditional Feel

The harsh beauty of the Louisiana swamplands lends itself perfectly to the plaintive music of the people and on Saturday nights the chirping of the crickets, the barking of the 'gators and the croaking of the fat-bellied bull-frogs, mingle with the raw, gutsy sounds of the Cajun fiddle, accordion and triangle.

By the mid-'70s, Cajun music was basically commercial dance music and its origins had been obscured by various outside influences but the traditional 'feel' of the 17th-century French settlers could still be detected in many of the songs.

One of the first artists to record Cajun music was Joe Falcon, an accordionist who began making discs in the late 1920's. The accordion enjoyed enormous popularity with Cajun musicians until the beginning of the '40s, when it almost completely disappeared from commercial recordings.

Now French language is what really identifies Cajun music but, until the early 1900's, the fiddle and triangle gave the songs an individual sound of their own. German settlers, who began making their homes in Louisiana at the end of the 19th century, brought with them accordions, and by the turn of the 20th century the washboard was being added to the line-up of certain Cajun bands to give added rhythm, but it wasn't until the '30s that the rhythm guitar began to be featured.

From the mid-'20s, record companies like RCA Victor, Paramount and Decca began taking an interest in the music but only after World War Two did Cajun really move outside the Louisiana boundaries and become fully accepted. During those early years countless numbers of local bands and solo musicians thrived. Among the most popular of these Cajun groups were the Hackberry Ramblers (consisting of Luderin Darbone on fiddle, Edwin Duhon on bass and Lennis Sonnier on guitar), Miller's Merrymakers, J. B. Fuselier, Leo Soileau and Happy Fats who, between them, produced such localized 'hits' as 'Step It Fast', 'Elton Two-Step', 'Hackberry Hop', 'Ponce A Moi' and 'Vain Ton Don A Ma Mort'.

Throughout the recorded history of Cajun music the fiddle has remained a predominant force, although during the first 20 years or so the German accordion was also popular as a lead instrument. By the 1950's, however, the fiddle began to take a subordinate position to the accordion whicn, by that time, had made a resounding comeback following a hit recording, 'Pine Grove Blues', by Nathan Abshire. With the additional help of other Cajun musicians like Iry Le Jeune and Lawrence Walker, the accordion was finally established as *the* instrument of Cajun music. Its status was further enhanced by a black musician, Cleveland Crochet, who recorded the highly successful 'Sugar Bee'.

From Swing To Hillbilly

The one song that firmly established Cajun on the open market was the traditional 'Jolie Blon' (Pretty Blonde), recorded in 1946 by the legendary Harry Choates, an outstanding French-fiddle player from New Iberia. Choates, who recorded for the independent Gold Star label in Houston, Texas, gave the music its first big hit and, following the success of 'Jolie Blon', numerous other companies began to record Cajun material, among them Macy's (who also issued Jim Reeves' first singles), Humming Bird and Imperial; but it was the actual Louisiana-based labels that ultimately benefited from Cajun's new-found popularity.

Harry Choates was probably the last of the great Cajun fiddle players for, by the 1950's, the accordion was firmly accepted by musicians and public alike and tiny record labels like Cajun Classics, La-Louisianne, Lanor and Khoury's began to build up their own individual catalogues of accordion music.

Right: Clifton Chenier, the noted blues accordion player who popularized Cajun.

The Nitty Gritty Dirt Band, the '70s exponents of Cajun-flavoured country music whose chart success gave Cajun a wider audience.

Western Swing, the dance craze that swept the Southern States of America during the '30s and '40s influenced certain of the less traditionally-inclined Acadian players and they adopted the steel guitar as a featured instrument, a factor which hastened the national acceptance of Cajun in later years.

The late '50s and early '60s saw the emergence of 'country' or 'hillbilly' Cajun music through the recordings of Jimmy 'C' Newman and Rusty and Doug Kershaw. Both Newman and the Kershaw brothers were born in Louisiana and were steeped in Acadian traditions, but it was possibly the success of Hank Williams's song 'Jambalaya (On The Bayou)' that prompted them to experiment with a more commercialized form of Louisiana French music.

Newman, from Big Mamou, recorded several traditional songs in the French language, including 'Jolie Blon', 'Grand Basile' and 'Grand Chenier', but his greatest successes were in the true modern country music style of the time. Rusty and Doug Kershaw, on the other hand, remained fairly faithful to their Cajun roots and recorded several tracks in the idiom.

In 1960, Doug Kershaw wrote the now classic 'Louisiana Man', released the

following year and subsequently 'covered' by no less than 900 other artists. Kershaw, whilst not fully accepted by fellow Louisiana musicians, became one of the great Cajun innovators of the '60s generation and, although he mostly wrote his own material, the backings on his albums were invariably traditional Cajun, with accordion, fiddle and triangle. Among Kershaw's better-known recorded works are 'Cajun Joe (The Bully Of The Bayou)', 'Fais Do Do', 'Dans La Louisianne', 'Colinda' (based on the calinda, an erotic dance originating in San Domingo and taken to Louisiana by black slaves), 'Bayou Teche' and 'Mama Rita In Hollywood'.

An interesting byproduct of Cajun is Zodico or Zydeco, created mainly by black musicians from a fusion of old French folk tunes, rhythm & blues and basic rock. Among the foremost exponents of Zodico music was Clifton Chenier, an artist noted for his outstanding blues-accordion sound. Chenier claimed to have been influenced by Amade Ardoin, who was apparently the first coloured artist to play the blues on the accordion.

Cajun, with its infectious beat and plaintive melodies, became increasingly popular outside Louisiana largely through the

efforts of a small band of dedicated enthusiasts, among them Eddie Shuler (owner of the prolific Goldband Record label and a one-time member of the Hackberry Ramblers), Iry Le Jeune (whose recordings of 'Calcasieu Waltz' and 'Teche Special' established him as one of the most popular of all Cajun accordionists) and Chris Strachwitz who was responsible for producing numerous Cajun albums by the Hackberry Ramblers, Clifton Chenier and the Louisiana Honeydrippers.

Cajun musicians number in their thousands and notable performers past and present include the Grand Mamou Orchestra, Bessyl Duhon, Willie Trahan, Dewey Balfa, the Branch Playboys, Link Davis, the Ardouin Brothers Orchestra, Nathan Abshire, Zozo Reynolds, Izeb Laza, Sidney Babineaux, Papa Cairo, Agnus LeJeune, the All Star Reveliers, the Rayne-Bo Ramblers, Aldus Roger and Jay Stutes.

A number of modern country bands introduced Cajun items into their repertoires in the late '60s and the early '70s, among them Buck Owens and the Buckeroos and the Nitty Gritty Dirt Band, but, in the main, Cajun was still the prized possession of the ancestors of the 10,000-strong French Acadians.

Hank Williams: The Hillbilly Shakespeare

Hank Williams, creator of some of the most harshly beautiful country ballads ever written, died a burned-out shell of a man at the age of 29. Williams, to use the title of an old country song, "lived hard, loved fast and died young." He was one of the greatest talents to emerge from the post-war period of American country music and so immense was his stature during his own lifetime that one admiring critic dubbed him the "hillbilly Shakespeare."

Born and raised on a run-down farm in Georgiana, Alabama, Williams was seven years old when he was first schooled in music by an old Negro street musician known as Tee-tot. This elderly 'busker' initiated Hank into the basic elements of the blues, a style that was to play an important part in the ultimate development of Williams's writing and singing in later years.

At the age of 12, Hank (Hiram) Williams sang one of his own compositions, 'WPA Blues' in a talent contest held at the Empire Theatre, Montgomery, and won a prize of $15. Within a very short space of time Hank had formed his own band, the Drifting Cowboys, which was successful enough to be given a regular spot on WSFA radio. Hank and the band remained with the station for a year, establishing something of a local record in broadcasting longevity.

Four years later Williams temporarily severed his connections in Montgomery and travelled to Texas, where he visited a rodeo and tried his hand at bronco busting. Drunk on cheap whisky, he was immediately thrown from a wild horse and sustained a severe spinal injury that was to plague him for the rest of his life.

Turning to alcohol and sedatives to minimize the pain from his damaged spine, Williams — already a naturally withdrawn and emotionally unstable personality — began to earn a reputation as a hell-raiser.

A stormy courtship and subsequent marriage to Audrey Shepherd stabilized the singer to some degree and it wasn't long before his songwriting ability came to the attention of Fred Rose, one half of the famous publishing team Acuff-Rose. Williams asked Rose to listen to a selection of songs he'd written. Rose heard the songs and was impressed enough to arrange for the young composer to record some titles for the Stirling label.

The first recording session, produced by Fred Rose, was on December 11, 1946 and Williams laid down four titles, 'Never Again (Will I Knock At Your Door)', 'Calling You', 'Wealth Won't Save Your Soul' and 'When God Comes And Gathers His Jewels'. A second session on February 13, 1947, produced a further four tracks, 'Honky Tonkin'', 'Pan American', 'I Don't Care (If Tomorrow Never Comes)' and 'My Love For You (Has Turned To Hate)'.

Recording Potential

Rose was already convinced of Williams's potential as a recording artist and decided to take him away from Stirling and seek a major label. Frank Walker, a former Columbia and later RCA Victor recording pioneer and talent scout, was at that time setting up a record label for Metro-Goldwyn-Mayer, so Rose contacted Walker with a view to recording Hank Williams for the new company. Four months after Hank's second and last session for the Stirling label, he went into the MGM studios and recorded 'Move It On Over', 'Last Night I Heard You Cryin' In Your Sleep' and 'On The Banks Of The Old Ponchartrain'.

'Move It On Over' became Hank Williams's first hit on MGM. It was to be the first of many hit recordings, most of them written by Hank himself, and they included 'Your Cheatin' Heart', 'I'm So Lonesome I Could Cry', 'Honky Tonk Blues', 'Kaw-Liga', 'Rootie Tootie', 'Cold, Cold Heart', 'Long Gone Lonesome Blues', 'A Mansion On The Hill', 'There'll Be No Teardrops Tonight', 'Jambalaya (On The Bayou)', 'Hey, Good Lookin'', 'Wedding Bells', 'Settin' The Woods On Fire', 'I Can't Help It', 'Half As Much', 'Take These Chains From My Heart', 'Lost Highway', 'Howlin' At The Moon', 'Window Shoppin'', 'Ramblin' Man' and possibly one of the biggest-selling 'hillbilly' records of all time, 'Lovesick Blues'.

One story gives an indication of Williams's unique ability as a songwriter. At the very beginning of his association with Fred Rose, Williams was asked to show some tangible proof of his songwriting talent. Presenting the artist with a hypothetical set of circumstances, Rose sent him into an adjoining office for 30 minutes and told Williams to compose a song. Hank emerged some twenty minutes later and handed Rose his test-piece, 'A Mansion On The Hill'. On April 12, 1948, Hank Williams signed his name to an exclusive Acuff-Rose songwriting contract.

During his brief life-span Hank Williams

Above: Careful studio shots like this revealed little of Hank's traumatic private life.

composed a total of 125 songs, many of which later became country and pop music standards. It took formidable inspiration to achieve so prolific an output. Like so many other rural American performers, Williams was steeped in religion and many of his songs took the form of inspirational pieces. Original compositions like 'I Saw The Light', 'I'm Going Home', 'Are You Building A Temple In Heaven' and 'The Angel Of Death' stand as powerful reminders of his rigid apocalyptic faith.

Williams was as versatile as he was prolific and under the archetypal pseudonym of Luke the Drifter, he recorded a series of moving and hard-hitting monologues for MGM, among them being 'Pictures From Life's Other Side', 'The Funeral', 'Men With Broken Hearts', 'Too Many Parties And Too Many Pals', 'Be Careful Of Stones That You Throw' and 'I Dreamed About Mom Last Night'. His raw, plaintive hillbilly voice made each one take on the flavour of a personal experience, which, indeed, it might have been.

Although the almost intolerable pain from Williams's damaged spine had no discernible effect on his recordings, it reflected appallingly on his personal life. His marriage to Audrey Shepherd, though it had provided some stability, was at its best a love-hate relationship and over the years his drinking became progressively worse.

Historic Night

Williams's reputation for hell-raising was so bad, even in the early days of his career, that Jim Denny, general manager for the *Grand Ole Opry*, refused to have him on the show. Later, however, the *Opry* management relented on the strength of his enormous popularity with the record-buying public and booked him to appear on June 11, 1949. Hank sang his most famous song, 'Lovesick Blues', on that historic night and the audience responded with no less than five encores. So great was the enthusiasm for Williams that Red Foley, the host for that particular section of the show, was forced to make a short speech in order to quell the excitement.

The next two years were perhaps the happiest of Williams's life. He became an 'overnight sensation' in the words of the

Stylistics' song, but he was unprepared for the wealth that followed. Many of his associates from that period claim Williams could never quite come to terms with his tremendous popularity, and he nursed a Dylan-like grudge against the society that had elevated him to such a position. Nevertheless, his three years as a member of the *Grand Ole Opry* cast had a stimulating effect on him and for a while the savage bouts of drinking were curtailed.

In the end his bitterness fought its way to the surface again and Williams left a trail of broken bottles, wrecked hotels and angry words behind him. Stories emerged from the *Opry* about his slanging matches with hecklers in the audience and his apparent inability to arrive for the show on time. His marriage to Audrey was nearing its end and in January, 1952, they finally parted. Eight months later, Jim Denny, who could tolerate Williams's erratic behaviour no longer, sacked him from the *Grand Ole Opry*. It was the beginning of the end.

Hank Williams left Nashville in disgrace but within a matter of weeks he'd met and married Billie Jean Jones in New Orleans. This union, too, ended in tragedy of the most final kind, for, on January 1, 1953, Hank Williams died in the back seat of his Cadillac on the way to a performance in Ohio. An element of mystery surrounds Williams's death. The medical report stated that he died from a heart attack but most of the singer's friends and colleagues firmly believe that a sedative, chloral hydrate (a powerful heart depressant), was the direct cause of death.

At the Ohio theatre where Williams was scheduled to appear on that night, a single light was focused onto the bare stage from the lighting gallery and a recording of Hank's immortal 'I Saw The Light' was played over the public address system. His body lay in state at Montgomery's Municipal Auditorium and more than 25,000 people lined the streets to attend the funeral. A local newspaper, *The Reporter*, described the final ceremony as being: "The greatest emotional orgy in the city's history since the inauguration of Jefferson Davis."

From his humble beginnings in a tumble-down log cabin in the backwoods of Alabama, Hank Williams had become a poet of the people, a creator of some of the most haunting musical dialogue ever written. Most of the great names in country music have common denominators of sincerity, audience rapport and humility, but none more so than Hank Williams.

Country-Pop Fusion

Williams left country music one of its greatest legacies of songs and its most colourful legend. Virtually unaided by outside influences, this lanky Alabama farmboy brought about the interchange and fusion between country and pop music which has since had such notable repercussions. His backing sound of steel guitar, fiddle and heavy pounding electric guitar was the undisputed forerunner of the Nashville Sound. Had he lived, claimed one writer, Hank Williams would very likely have precipitated considerably the acceptance of country music in the big metropolitan cities.

Jimmie Rodgers was among the first country artists to popularize country music on a national scale but Hank Williams brought it to the attention of Tin Pan Alley and artists like Tony Bennett, Tommy Edwards, Joni James, Guy Mitchell and Ray Charles. In more recent years that list has extended to the Carpenters, Linda Ronstadt, Frank Ifield and a host of others outside of the country music field. Within the actual structure of country music, the songs of Hank Williams have become a part of America's rich musical heritage, being performed by almost every artist on the country scene.

Some years after his death Metro-Goldwyn-Mayer attempted to embellish the Hank Williams legend by producing a film entitled *Your Cheatin' Heart*, starring George Hamilton, with the voice of Williams's own son, Hank Williams Jnr., performing most of the songs. The result was a tawdry, badly produced but mercifully brief example of exploitational cinema at its worst. It depicted Williams as an alcoholic, thrill-seeking extrovert with a flair for songwriting. The true legend of Hank Williams is contained in the 125 songs he composed during a lifetime fraught with pain, emotional suffering and a guilt complex about an artistic status he felt he didn't deserve.

Below: George Hamilton as Hank Williams in the movie *Your Cheatin' Heart*.

Ronald Grant

Jim Reeves: Country Gent

The words engraved on the bronze plaque exhibited in Nashville's Country Music Hall of Fame are as follows: ''Jim Reeves. August 20, 1924, to July 31, 1964. The velvet style of Gentleman Jim Reeves was an international influence. His rich voice brought millions of new fans to country music from every corner of the world. Although the crash of his private airplane in 1964 took his life . . . posterity will keep his name alive . . . because they will remember him as one of country music's most important performers.''

The son of an impoverished Texas farming family, Reeves had been a very successful country music recording artist before he actually came to the attention of the world at large. It wasn't until he signed a recording contract with RCA Victor in 1955, under the guidance of Steve Sholes (and later Chet Atkins), however, that the now familiar Reeves 'sound' began to emerge. It was a sound – that is, a combination of vocal and instrumental sounds – that virtually reshaped the course of modern country music.

Whilst pop music pundits attach scant importance to Reeves's recorded works, there can be little or no doubt that, in his own uniquely individual way, this ex-hillbilly 'novelty' vocalist contributed as much to the overall acceptance of country music in the '60s, as did Jimmie Rodgers some 30 years earlier.

Simplicity was the key to Reeves's astounding latterday success. In the place of his earlier dyed-in-the-wool country style came a sound that was more commercially acceptable. The old fast-paced 'novelty' songs were swept aside with the signing of the Victor contract and Reeves's rich baritone, hitherto unused on disc, was exploited to the full.

Countless writers have attempted to analyze the outstanding success of Jim Reeves but few, if any, have been able to explain it fully. Certainly he possessed a uniquely warm voice and he was able to bring a touch of credibility to the most mundane lyrics. Reeves could make the old Tin Pan Alley 'Moon, June and Spoon' clichés sound intimate and personal.

Perhaps the true explanation lies in the fact that Reeves happened to find the right songs and a sympathetic recording company at a time when the world was tiring of the raucous cacophony of sounds produced by the pop groups of that era. The general public had already bitten at the country music cake through the recordings of Johnny Horton, Leroy Van Dyke, the Browns, Hank Locklin and Eddy Arnold, and when Jim Reeves happened on the scene he merely provided the icing.

Big Break

In 1952, Reeves began recording for the Texas-based Macy's Queen of Hits record company, producing four sides, 'Teardrops Of Regret', 'My Heart's Like A Welcome Mat', 'Chicken Hearted Me' and 'I've Never Been So Blue'. The songs, issued as two singles, sold through the company's chain-stores and were strictly regional successes but they gave Reeves the encouragement he needed to pursue a singing career. At that time he was a station announcer and disc-jockey with radio KGRI, in Henderson, Texas. Reeves's vocal style in those days was in keeping with the nasal, high-pitched singing characteristic of that period. Reeves was also known professionally as Sonny Day and under this appropriately-chosen pseudonym he played a number of engagements in and around New Mexico with a small back-up band.

That same year Reeves, now married to Mary White, decided to move to Shreveport, Louisiana, where he took a job with KWKH, the station featuring the famed *Louisiana Hayride*. It was Reeves's task to

announce the country programme every Saturday night and, on rare occasions, he was allowed to sing over the air. The artist's big break came when he was asked to deputize for Hank Williams on the *Hayride*, when the latter failed to appear. Abbott recording boss Fabor Robinson, who happened to be in the audience that evening, heard Reeves and immediately signed him to a contract with his label.

Jim Reeves's first release for Abbot, 'Wagon Of Love', passed by almost unnoticed but the next single, 'Mexican Joe', penned by fellow Abbott artist Mitchell Torok, sold over a million copies and reputedly earned Reeves a gold disc. The follow-up, 'Bimbo', was also a hit and provided Jim with his second million-seller and alleged accompanying gold record. Whilst numerous American publications of the day credited the singer with these two gold discs, they were never actually presented to him.

In all Jim Reeves recorded a total of 36 songs for Abbott, all of which were later sold to RCA Victor, who subsequently issued the majority on budget albums. The remaining five or six titles, which were reputed to be very 'raw' in delivery and overall production, remained in RCA's vaults and seemed unlikely ever to emerge.

With the success of 'Mexican Joe', Reeves was invited to become a regular performer on the *Hayride* and he remained with the show for over two years, appearing with such notables as Hank Williams, Zeke Clements, Betty Amos and Goldie Hill.

Reeves's singles for Abbott resulted in numerous enquiries from other larger recording companies and in 1955, he signed with RCA. Almost immediately he hit the country charts with his own composition, 'Yonder Comes A Sucker', a song based on an older folk ballad, 'Railroad, Steamboat (River And Canal)'. Two more hits, 'According To My Heart' and 'My Lips Are Sealed' followed in rapid succession, as a result of which — at the express recommendation of no less than Ernest Tubb and Hank Snow — Reeves was invited to become a member of the cast of the *Grand Ole Opry*, America's longest-running radio show. Other artists on the *Opry*'s impressive roster then included Lester Flatt and Earl Scruggs, Stonewall Jackson, Bill Monroe, Jimmie Driftwood, Wilma Lee and Stoney Cooper, Jimmy 'C' Newman, Faron Young and Porter Wagoner.

In 1957, 'Four Walls', a sentimental country ballad composed by Marvin Moore and George Campbell, climbed into the British hit parade, giving the record-buying public a foretaste of what was to come. 'Four Walls' introduced the new Reeves sound of piano, electric bass and acoustic guitar. Reeves' producer, Chet Atkins, also worked on the singer's voice and developed a close-to-the-mike technique that gave it greater clarity and warmth. It was a formula that RCA was to adhere to throughout the remainder of Jim Reeves's stay with the label.

Slowly but very surely Jim Reeves became a worldwide star, with particular emphasis on Great Britain and South Africa. Virtually every single released by RCA entered the country charts, many of them crossing over into the pop field. Among Reeves' most popular recordings were 'Blue Boy' (September '58), 'He'll Have To Go' (February '60), 'Am I Losing You' (January '61), 'Danny Boy' (May '61), 'Adios Amigo' (July '62), 'Welcome To My World' (May '63), 'Guilty' (October '63), 'I Love You Because' (February '64), 'I Won't Forget You' (June '64), 'There's A Heartache Following Me' (October '64), 'It Hurts So Much' (January '65), 'Is It Really Over' (October '65), 'Distant Drums' (August '66), 'I Won't Come In While He's There' (January '67), and 'But You Love Me Daddy' (November '69).

Comfort Through Sorrow

Reeves's hits weren't always instant chart entries; many of them, including the resonant 'Distant Drums', originally scheduled for a much earlier release but postponed for what amounted to political reasons relating directly to America's Vietnam War commitment, sold steadily over a period of weeks — even months — before eventually entering the best-selling charts. Most of Jim's songs — and he composed many himself — centred around a theme of lost love, so beloved by country writers. The lyrics were always simple and direct and set down in a way that the public could instantly identify with. It could even be said Reeves spoke a message of comfort through his saddest songs; in every one the backing was totally subordinated to his rich, appealing voice.

In 1962 Jim Reeves toured South Africa, where his popularity was enormous, and it proved to be the focal point for even greater success in the British Isles. Reeves made such a tremendous impact

Right: Jim with a chorus line-up in the period movie *Kimberley Jim*.

Aquarius

newspapers everywhere gave the disaster front-page coverage. The country music industry, still not fully recovered from the equally violent deaths the previous year of Patsy Cline, Hawkshaw Hawkins, Cowboy Copas and Jack Anglin, reeled under the blow.

While Reeves's countless fans greeted the news of his death with an almost eerie calmness, the master-cult that sprang up within a year of the plane crash could be compared to the near-hysteria surrounding the deaths of Rudolph Valentino and James Dean. As late as a decade after his death the Reeves legend showed little sign of fading, and Mary Reeves continued to preserve her late husband's 'Gentlemen Jim' image zealously, being careful to ensure — as with royalty — that only the 'right' publicity was released to the waiting reporters. Amusing offbeat anecdotes emanating from Nashville about Jim's liking for Jack Daniels bourbon whisky were quietly suppressed, and Reeves gradually emerged for posterity as a musical deity.

Mystic Charisma

Although Jim Reeves never possessed visual sex appeal of the most obvious kind — he even wore a toupee to conceal his rapidly receding hairline — his musical persona embodied a strange charisma and mystique that drew out the maternal instincts in his thousands of female followers. He seemed able to invest even the most banal song with a poignancy and sincerity that made it timeless, and his tactfully guarded image — the smiling country gentleman — enshrined these qualities.

RCA, in conjunction with Mary Reeves, astutely guided the release of the late singer's last-recorded albums and singles throughout the world, resulting in an even greater upsurge of popularity outside the country music field. At one period no less than nine Jim Reeves albums appeared in the British charts! A number of unissued tracks still remained in the vaults, comprised of Forces Recruiting recordings made in Nashville's WSM studios, several homemade demonstration tapes and the residue of the 36 titles Reeves cut for the Abbott label. Whether these songs would ever emerge was open to speculation, but in view of the re-cycling policy in constant operation for Reeves's more than substantial general catalogue, it seemed extremely unlikely.

Devotees of the more traditional forms of American country music — which was enjoying an upsurge in popularity by the mid-'70s — adamantly insist that Jim Reeves was never a true 'son of the soil' because of his clear commercial influences. Be that as it may, it would be foolish to ignore the tremendous influence Reeves has had on the music industry as a whole. A living force long after his early death, he probably brought country and country-orientated songs to more people across the world than any other singer in the history of popular music.

on the South African people that he returned a year later to star in *Kimberley Jim,* a film based on the diamond strike at the turn of the century. It was Reeves's first and only film. Whilst *Kimberley Jim* met with little critical acclaim, it was a huge box-office success and a rough draft for a second film, also with a South African setting, was drawn up but Reeves died before the script could be finalized.

Reeves loved South Africa and its people and during his second visit he recorded several songs in the Afrikaans language. Reeves at one point told Gilbert Gibson, one of the songwriters commissioned to write material for *Kimberley Jim,* that he eventually hoped to settle in that country.

In the spring of 1964, Jim Reeves and his group, the Blue Boys, toured Scandinavia, Austria, Germany, Holland, Italy and Ireland with Chet Atkins, Bobby Bare and the Anita Kerr Singers. That Jim Reeves was already a legend was confirmed by the thousands of cheering fans who greeted him in each of the countries he visited. The tour was a great success for all concerned, particularly Jim Reeves, and when it was over he flew to England to promote his current hit recording, 'I Love You Because' on television.

Not only was Jim Reeves a pheno-menally successful recording artist, he was also a shrewd businessman in a number of spheres. A large proportion of his earnings were derived from his own publishing companies, Tuckahoe, Open Road and Acclaim, and in addition to signing his compositions to them, Reeves endeavoured to contract the works of other writers to the publishing houses.

Real estate was another of Reeves's business interests and it was whilst on a flight from Batesville, Arkansas, to Nashville, following the negotiation of a property deal, that the single-engined Beechcraft airplane rented by Dean Manuel (Reeves' pianist and manager) and piloted by Reeves crashed. The plane, with its two occupants, Reeves and Manuel, was about to land at Nashville's Berry Field airport, when radio contact was lost. A search party numbering some 400 people, among them such names as Stonewall Jackson, Marty Robbins, Eddy Arnold and Chet Atkins, set out in a blinding rainstorm to scour the dense woodland surrounding the airfield and its approaches.

During the afternoon of August 2, 1964, the wreckage of the light aircraft was discovered by the search party. Jim Reeves and Dean Manuel were both dead.

The world was stunned at the news of the star's tragic death, and national

Johnny Cash

Of his phenomenal success, Johnny Cash wryly commented: "Success is having to worry about every damned thing in the world except money."

In the '60s, though, it was a different story: Cash earned himself a reputation for being unreliable because of his dependence on pills. He reckoned the toughest fight of his life was finally kicking the habit. The realization came after spending a night in gaol and not knowing how he got there.

Cash grew up in the traditional manner of country artists, knowing hunger, poverty and the personal tragedy of seeing his brother killed in an accident on the farm. The toughness of his earlier life manifested itself frequently in the songs he wrote. His success wasn't achieved overnight, although his name was revered in country music circles for decades.

It was thanks to his brother Roy, who was insistent upon visiting a country show at Overton Park Shell, in Memphis, Tennessee, that Johnny Cash decided to pursue a full-time career in music.

Cash's fan club magazine *Strictly Cash* recalled the singer's first telephone conversation in 1955 with the legendary Sam Phillips of Sun Records: "Mr. Phillips, my name is John Cash. I write songs and play the guitar and I wonder if you would listen to me?"

Phillips, however, gave a negative reply but suggested that Cash call again in two weeks. Almost a month elapsed before Cash finally secured an audition with Sun, but during the interim period he and two friends, Marshal Grant and Luther Perkins — the Tennessee Two — rehearsed with

relentless determination.

Their repertoire consisted mainly of spirituals, hymns and a few ballads that Cash himself had written over the years.

When the audition day finally came around, Cash and his two friends stood before Phillips and performed song after song without arousing the slightest reaction from the one-man 'panel'. Finally, Phillips asked the trio to play a further selection, and from these he chose one of Cash's own compositions, 'Hey Porter', to make the A side of the group's first record. Although they lacked a coupling title, Cash rectified the situation that same evening by writing a 'love ballad' (as Phillips called it), titled 'Cry, Cry, Cry'.

Instant Success

This first release proved to be a big seller and Cash followed it with such songs as 'Folsom Prison Blues', 'I Walk The Line', 'There You Go', 'Don't Make Me Go', 'Home Of The Blues' and 'Ballad Of A Teenage Queen'.

Cash's instant but, nevertheless, restricted success on record was due, in the main, to the unique sound produced by Marshal Grant and Luther Perkins — a sound that stripped a song to its soul and rebuilt it around a hard-driving, thumping rockabilly beat, over-ridden by Cash's gravelly vocals.

Later, with the added services of drummer W. S. Holland, the group became known as Johnny Cash and the Tennessee Three, and their already distinctive sound became even more pronounced. Cash slowly but very surely gained the respect of a wider audience and his songs like 'I Walk The Line' were being picked up by artists outside the country belt.

Years later Cash recalled those early Sun days with fondness: "Like I said, I've always loved to sing. Somewhere, locked in the vaults of Sun Records, are some tapes I did with Elvis Presley back in the days when we were beginning to grow together with Sam Phillips. I think we sang some hymns on those sessions. I seem to remember Elvis playing piano and the two of us singing 'The Old Rugged Cross' and 'Peace In the Valley'. I sure would like to listen to them again some day."

After recording a further 13 hit singles for Sun, Cash and his band moved to the Columbia stable and began to produce such classics as 'Don't Take Your Guns To Town', 'I Got Stripes', 'Smilin' Bill McCall', 'Frankie's Man Johnny', 'Seasons Of My Heart', 'Goin' To Memphis', 'Locomotive Man', 'Forty Shades Of Green', 'Tennessee Flat-Top Box' and 'Big River'.

Suddenly, there followed a sharp decline in popularity for Cash and a period that produced a series of mediocre recordings. Just when the country music world was beginning to contemplate Cash's future, the singer came bouncing back with 'Ring Of Fire', a song written by June Carter and Merle Kilgore. This single, which made the charts in 1963, was by way of an experimental departure from Cash's characteristic sound in that it incorporated a Tijuana-style brass section. It was as though Cash had deliberately defied country music convention by daring to use trumpets — but it worked, providing him with his biggest hit to date and establishing him in the pop and country charts.

This was the beginning of the Cash legend, although the foundations had already been laid during the previous decade with Sun.

In the wake of 'Ring Of Fire' came 'The Matador', again featuring a Mexican brass sound, 'Understand Your Man' (with its characteristic dobro and trumpet coupling), 'The Ballad Of Ira Hayes' and 'It Ain't Me, Babe'.

With the latter recording, Cash's friendship and musical associations with folk doyen Bob Dylan began to receive wide publicity in trendy pop journals and Johnny slowly became accepted by America's folk legions. It was strongly rumoured at the time that Cash, seeking to identify not only with an already loyal country audience but to cultivate a rapport between himself and the urban folk revival, wandered unannounced and unheralded into a Greenwich Village, New York, coffee bar, a haunt of both folk devotees and

Johnny Cash appearing with Peter Falk in an episode of the popular TV series *Colombo*. Below: Johnny Cash and Dylan in the film *Johnny Cash, The Man And His Music*.

performers alike, sang a few ethnic ballads and wandered straight back out again. The story, true or otherwise, made an indelible impression on America's folk contingent and they quickly identified with this amiable but unpredictable giant called Johnny Cash.

On Friday, August 2, 1968, Luther Perkins, the mainstay of the Cash band, received burns from which he subsequently died. Cash and the remainder of his show who, at that time numbered the Carter Family, the Statler Brothers and ex-Sun 'rocker' Carl Perkins, were stunned by the tragedy and for a time it seemed that the Cash 'sound' might be lost forever. Carl Perkins, however, stood in for some weeks until Cash was able to find a musician capable of recreating Luther Perkins' guitar sound. The replacement proved to be a highly competent guitarist by the name of Bob Wooten. Cash, in fact, asserted that Perkins would never be replaced: "We may find someone to stand in for Luther but he will never be replaced."

Cash's involvement in various social causes, including prison reform and the plight of the American Indians, added to his popularity as an entertainer. An early album, 'Bitter Tears', the material of which was written in collaboration with the late Peter LeFarge, was solely devoted to the Indian cause. Two later recordings, 'Johnny Cash At Folsom Prison' (1968) and 'Johnny Cash At San Quentin' (1969), proved to be among the most outstanding live albums ever released.

Pioneer Image

The San Quentin album provided Cash with the most successful single of his entire career, 'A Boy Named Sue', written by *Playboy* cartoonist Shel Silverstein. It was a world-wide hit for Cash in 1969 and he received a Grammy for the Best Country Male Vocal Performance and a Country Music Association Accolade for the Best Single Of The Year.

By this time Cash's reputation as a rugged and hard-hitting rebel with a past had reached a crescendo and the press made a great play of his terms in jail and of his battle-scarred face. To the press and the rest of the world Johnny Cash symbolized the last bastions of the old frontier days. In point of fact Cash, in spite of his previous involvement with soft drugs had only spent a couple of nights in jail, one on a charge of illegally possessing pills in El Paso, and the other for illegally picking flowers! Cash dedicated a song, 'Starkville City Jail', to the latter incident and included it on his historic 'San Quentin' album. The deep scar on the left side of his face was the direct result of a cyst and not, as legend would have it, a knife thrust or bullet wound.

Shortly after the Starkville City prison chapter, Cash managed to shake off his pill habit with a little help from his friends, and a new era began. Cash began to involve himself in religion.

"I've always been a deeply religious person," he said at the time, "but now the light's shining a little brighter than it did a few years ago. I've had a lot of straightening out to do in the past and I wasn't always honest about it but that's over now, thanks to June (June Carter Cash — his second wife) and the good friends who've always stood by me."

Brief Obsession

Religion became something of an obsession with Cash for a brief period and he formed a friendly liaison with evangelist Billy Graham. At one stage, following the release of an album entitled 'The Gospel Road', the dialogue of which was recorded in the Holy Land, it seemed that Cash might turn his back on country music altogether and devote the remainder of his life to preaching the gospel.

Johnny Cash and country music stayed together, though, and while the hit records weren't quite as regular as they had been he remained the undisputed king of country music.

"People like my songs because there's realism in them, unlike most songs," he said. "They have true human emotions as well as being real stories. My music is more of a personal thing than a vehicle to use to carry messages. It's mainly something to be enjoyed. I sing songs and do the job I'm cut out to do." A simple view, but one which has enabled Cash to maintain his phenomenal success.

The inimitable Johnny Cash with his wife, June Carter of Carter Family fame.

Tammy Wynette

Tammy Wynette is part of the legend that is Nashville, Tennessee. She has been possibly the most successful of all female country artists. Her appeal was not merely confined to the collectors of country recordings but reached out to embrace college kids, rock buffs and general middle-of-the-road devotees. Tammy, with her soulful, emotion-charged voice, gave America's womenfolk an ambassador, a spokesman to echo their hopes and fears through the lyrics of a hundred songs. Tammy Wynette had been called 'America's First Lady', and it's a title she wore with grace and dignity.

In the few short years since she first became a recording artist, Tammy Wynette had over 20 singles in the no. 1 slot in the country charts, and her world-wide hit, 'Stand By Your Man', was the biggest single by a woman in the entire history of country music.

Unknown Gamble

Tammy's discovery by producer Billy Sherrill is almost a legend in itself. For the first time in his career Sherrill was tempted to take a gamble on an unknown artist. At that time he had only been into country music for a short period, having been a sax player in an R&B band in Alabama and a mixer for Sam Phillips's Sun label. Sherrill had grown up detesting country music and all it stood for, but as a producer for Epic records had come to acknowledge that there was money to be

made from what he called 'white sugar'.

Sherrill had been encouraged by the success of David Houston's 'Almost Persuaded', which became a Grammy-winner in 1966, and he was anxious to lay into some more heart-rending, lushly-produced modern country. When Tammy Wynette waltzed into Sherrill's office in 1966, he was basically unimpressed by what she had to offer, but a certain quality in her voice suggested that there were vague possibilities.

After hawking her voice and a few self-penned songs round all the major labels and receiving rejections, Tammy considered Billy Sherrill and Epic Records to be a last resort. Her job in an Alabama beauty parlour was still open and she had the added responsibility of raising three children. Sherrill didn't like Tammy's songs but he decided to take a chance on her voice. It had the kind of quality that he

needed to emulate the success of Houston's weeper and because he felt sorry for her, Sherrill gave Tammy a song called 'Apartment Number 9', written by Johnny Paycheck and Bobby Austin.

Tammy was raised on a farm in Mississippi and had married at the age of 17. Three years and three children later she was divorced. Her background leaked out to the press and hundreds of thousands of women all over America identified with her so that when 'Apartment Number 9' was released in 1966, it became an instant success. Sherrill's initial gamble with Tammy amounted to about one hour's worth of studio time at Epic but the first single quickly justified his faith in her.

The second disc, 'Your Good Girl's Gonna Go Bad', penned by Sherrill and Glenn Sutton, went to no. 1 in 1967 and was followed by an incredible 15 consecutive no. 1 country hits, including 'Stand By Your Man', 'D-I-V-O-R-C-E', 'It's All Over' (with David Houston) and 'Take Me To Your World'.

Blind Faith

Tammy's belief in Sherrill was total. "If he came in and told me to record 'Yankee Doodle', I'd do it," she is on record as saying. "A lot of people in Nashville think Billy is a son-of-a-bitch, but others, including me, look upon him as a genius. As a producer he is without equal, and everything he writes — which is about 50 songs up to now — turns to instant gold."

Sherrill had a reputation for being uncommunicative and difficult to work with, but according to Tammy: "He's a very shy, introverted kind of person and he takes a lot of getting to know."

In the studio, Sherrill had the reputation for always being right and on numerous occasions he upset artists like Tammy by insisting that certain things were done his way.

"There was a time," she recalled, "when Billy came out of the control room and suggested that I talked the line of a song. Now I don't like that kind of thing and I didn't think it would work but I finally went ahead and did it just like Billy said and it worked. Another time he wanted me to cut the old Johnny Ray song 'Cry' and I argued that it wasn't my kind of material. It was the only time that I have actually argued with Billy. I really did say 'no' on that one, but he persuaded me to try it and it turned out to be such a good sound. Billy was right. He always is. I don't think I could ever record without Billy. He's been with me from the very beginning of my career."

Although Tammy began to develop her talents as a songwriter and included one or two on her albums, it was Sherrill who made the final decisions as to the selection of material. Some of Tammy's biggest successes were written by Sherrill himself, including 'I Don't Wanna Play House',

The stage confidence that managed to survive the traumas of a broken marriage.

Tammy's songs hit right home to the country soap opera belt of women who struggled from dawn until dusk with household chores, kids, brunches, lunches and evening meals. Each one of them knew that Tammy was singing from personal experience and the songs gave them something to identify with. Songs like 'I Don't Wanna Play House', 'Stand By Your Man', 'What A Man My Man Is', 'Stayin' Home Woman', 'D-I-V-O-R-C-E' and 'My Man', made Tammy Wynette the new 'Queen Of Country Music', a title once bestowed on Kitty Wells.

Tammy's stormy marriage to country star George Jones gave her already hugely successful recording career an additional boost. Sherrill began producing George's sessions when the artist joined the Epic roster and inevitably he cut a lot of material with Tammy. A number of superb duets emerged during the happier period of their marriage and Sherrill was kept busy creating hit recordings for three separate but united entities, Tammy Wynette, George Jones and George Jones and Tammy Wynette. Among the most popular duets recorded by this formidable husband and wife team were 'Let's Build A World Together', 'We're Gonna Hold On' and '(We're Not The) Jet Set'.

Country Queen

Tammy's marriage to George Jones ended in divorce and all that's left to remind the world that these two country giants were once husband and wife are a series of albums produced by Sherrill.

"I guess my career could have been seriously affected by the breakup, because I used to rely so much on George on stage. I have never been fully at ease with audiences on my own and it took quite a lot of inner courage to convince myself that I could make it on my own again. Luckily George allowed me to retain his old band, the Jones Boys — he'd used them for 15 years — when we finally split, and that made things a lot easier," Tammy commented.

Tammy Wynette was destined to keep her 'Queen of Country Music' title for many years. Her crystal clear voice and sophisticated phrasing, coupled with the genius of Sherrill's production techniques, made her 'America's First Lady' of country music. It seemed that as long as she remained with Billy Sherrill the hits would keep on coming. Even if Sherrill happened to part company with Epic Records, Tammy had a clause in her ten-year contract giving her the right to use Sherrill independently.

The wounds sustained from her final breakup with George Jones finally healed and she viewed song titles like 'D-I-V-O-R-C-E', 'We're Gonna Hold On', 'Let's Build A World Together' and 'We're Putting It Back Together' with a certain wry smile.

"It seems like my whole life has been mapped out for me in the songs I sing," said Tammy, "and it's more than a little uncanny."

'Singing My Song' and 'It's All Over', but other writers like Jerry Chesnut, Curley Putman, Jan Crutchfield, Glenn Sutton (another top Epic producer and the husband of Lynn Anderson), Dave Loggins and Norro Wilson, contributed greatly to her overall popularity.

Much of Tammy's overwhelming popularity with female country fans was entirely due to the fact that the Women's Liberation movement simply didn't appeal to them. The very titles of some of

George Hamilton IV: The Country Ambassador

George Hamilton IV was something of a musical enigma. In the States, where country music enjoyed such a vast and dedicated following, he didn't rate too highly in the national popularity stakes, though his singles frequently made the country charts. Britain, however, while almost reluctant to fully accept country music, afforded Hamilton the status of a star.

Other American country performers entered the British pop charts on many occasions but few managed to sustain the public's interest for any length of time. Hamilton, on the other hand, built up a lasting popularity and though the reason for that was hard to analyze, much of it could easily have been attributed to a brilliant public relations campaign.

There was more to Hamilton than bland singing and clever publicity, though both factors were fairly relevant. He was a typical American 'nice guy' but with him it was no phoney image designed to offset a lack of talent. He was a homely, slow-talking North Carolinan possessing an ability to make friends, and he rarely forgot a name or face.

The clever publicity surrounding Hamilton was the very lack of it. No racy or even remotely controversial stories were circulated by the press and it was that, coupled with the singer's stable public image, that endeared him to so many people inside and outside the States.

Early Trier

Born in Winston-Salem in 1937 Hamilton came from a middle-class background, the type not usually associated with country music. However from his early childhood he displayed more than a passing interest in the music of Hank Williams and Ernest Tubb, and by the time he was 12 had made 'professional' overtures to the *Grand Ole Opry* management.

When Hamilton was older and able to appreciate the inner complexities of country music, rock & roll was having a disastrous effect on the entire country industry, resulting in a massive cut-back of products by rural artists; but after several abortive attempts to break into the recording business Hamilton was finally able to persuade Orville Campbell, an executive with Colonial Records, to give him a contract.

Conscious of the waning popularity of country music at that time Hamilton recorded a pop song for his debut. The song, 'A Rose And A Baby Ruth', written by John D. Loudermilk, was trite but appealing and became a million-seller in 1956.

Two years later Hamilton signed with the larger ABC-Paramount and recorded 'Why Don't They Understand', composed by Joe 'Mr Piano' Henderson, a British writer and artist. The ballad became Hamilton's second million-seller.

For commercial reasons Hamilton had been obliged to record two pop songs, but

Below: Already a star, George Hamilton at the age of 21 (right) on holiday with his parents and his younger brother Cabot.

The relaxed appeal of a professional.

when the fad for rock & roll began to diminish he was able to change musical directions and sing country material. His first such song, 'Before This Day Ends', was penned by Roy Drusky, Vic McAlpin and Marie Wilson and reached no. 3 in the nation's country music charts in 1960.

The same year, Hamilton left ABC-Paramount and signed with RCA Victor under the direction of Chet Atkins. Country music was beginning to regain some of its lost ground and Hamilton was able to remain in that field, his first two hits for the company being 'Three Steps To The Phone' and 'Before This Day Ends', written by Harlan Howard and Vic McAlpin respectively.

The Howard song had been specially written for Jim Reeves who had scored heavily with 'He'll Have To Go', but because of the similarity of the two songs

32

Reeves had rejected it. It was destined for the waste basket in Atkins's office until Hamilton asked to hear the demo, liked it and recorded it.

His initial popularity with pop audiences had tapered off and he found himself establishing a workable rapport with American country devotees. His early songs for RCA were lightweight, easy on the ear and basically forgettable and it wasn't until 1962, when he recorded 'Abilene' (another of Loudermilk's efforts) that Hamilton's material took on any substance.

'Abilene' was a typical wistful country love song but it had more depth and meaning than most of the recordings of that period. It became a huge crossover pop-country hit for Hamilton, but most of all it was significant for its flavour, an indication of the singer's future musical direction.

As critic David Redshaw noted in

Country Music Review: ''George Hamilton IV was not yet into urban folk music though it was to eventually be the dominant influence on him, but he was beginning to delve into the folk roots of country and his albums included traditional tunes such as 'Roving Gambler', 'Come All Ye Fair And Tender Ladies' and the Carter Family standard, 'Jimmy Brown The Newsboy' — all done with tasteful, though not authentic, backing.''

Dallas, 1963

Good taste had been the hallmark of Hamilton's appeal as an artist and there were few other country artists who maintained such a flawless persona. Following 'Abilene' was a 'customized' ballad entitled 'Forth Worth, Dallas Or Houston', again written by Loudermilk. Originally recorded in 1963, the song was held over

Above: George Hamilton IV in London for another of his successful UK tours; (inset) the family man relaxes at home with his wife Tinky and their three children.

breaking into the country charts on a twice-yearly basis and the majority of his recordings from the mid-'60s and into the '70s adhered to the folk-country formula, his affinity with Canada and its composers becoming marked in later years.

After the successful 'Steel Rail Blues' came another Loudermilk song, 'Break My Mind', and then a return to folk with the classic Joni Mitchell composition, 'Urge For Going'. Many of Hamilton's friends in Nashville advised him against the song, suggesting that his fans wouldn't accept a number so far removed from the country field, but he ignored their warnings, cut the song in '67 and it climbed into the Top 10. He later considered the song to have been a forerunner of the folk-orientated 'Gentle On My Mind'-type songs that became so prominent at the turn of the '70s.

Royalty Bonus

Hamilton's career had been successful enough for him to pick and choose his material without too much regard for what was in vogue. If a song suited his voice he recorded it and worried more about the overall results of the actual session than the resultant sales. This attitude to financial gain was typical of the man who was dubbed 'International Ambassador of Country Music' — Hamilton lived for his music, but if a royalty cheque happened to be at the end of it, then so much the better.

He appeared to have no burning ambitions outside the country music industry though an appearance in a low-budget pop movie, *Hootennany Hoot*, during the early '60s indicated that he might develop a desire for acting when his popularity as a singing star waned. The film, however, was quickly forgotten and Hamilton was happy to let his career as a country singer develop.

His records were augmented by successful appearances on many top-rated American TV shows hosted by leading personalities like Jimmy Dean, Patti Page, Perry Como, Dick Clark and Steve Allen. In 1959 he began hosting his own ABC-TV show and the same year was invited to join the cast of the *Grand Ole Opry*.

Hamilton was the antithesis of the American showbiz personality and for that reason the role of superstar was well outside his grasp. In a career which, by 1975, had lasted almost 25 years, he enjoyed constant popularity by simply being himself.

Britain became almost a second home to Hamilton where he was an avid supporter of the anglicized country music scene and its smattering of contemporary composers. His relationship with the BBC resulted in a number of pleasant country-oriented TV series on BBC-2 and a staunch army of fans.

Further exposure in Britain via regular appearances at the annual International Festival of Country Music and several sell-out concert tours earned George Hamilton IV the right to be called as much if not more of a star in Britain as in the States.

until the following year because of the assassination of President Kennedy. RCA officials and Hamilton considered the reference to Dallas to be in bad taste at the time, but when it was eventually issued the record did extremely well in the country charts.

Hamilton's entry into the realms of contemporary folk music came two years later when he recorded Gordon Lightfoot's 'Early Morning Rain'. On the liner notes of his 'The Best Of George Hamilton IV' album Hamilton made the following comments about Canadian-born Lightfoot.

"This is one of my very favourite songs. It was written by my good friend Gordon Lightfoot, the great Canadian folk singer-composer. I could go on and on, but I'll just say that Mr. Lightfoot has been quite an influence on my career and was the inspiration for the folk-country style in which I have

been recording in recent years. I've recorded about a dozen Lightfoot tunes, but this is one of his classics."

The folk-country style, as Hamilton described it, was to become his identifying sound for the latter half of the '60s, but it was hardly original. Artists like Bobby Bare had successfully combined the two styles as far back as 1963, while the late Johnny Horton had carved a permanent niche for himself almost half a decade earlier when he recorded the traditionally-based 'Battle Of New Orleans'. Bare and Horton possessed earthy country voices, more suited to heavily rhythmic material, whereas Hamilton's light tenor style was in sympathy with the fragile construction of Lightfoot's material.

Hamilton selected another Lightfoot song as the follow-up to 'Early Morning Rain' — 'Steel Rail Blues'. By now he was

Waylon Jennings: The Nashville Rebel

Waylon Jennings's refusal to conform to the rigid demands of the Nashville establishment earned him a reputation as a rebel and at one period during his career he was actually dubbed "the Nashville Rebel." From relatively humble beginnings in Littlefield, Texas, where he was born in June, 1937, and a brief spell playing guitar for Buddy Holly, Jennings weathered the storm of protest about his dress and attitudes to country music and emerged as a cult figure.

His acceptance extended into rock circles, Jennings having long expressed a wish to record a rock album. In 1974 he and former Crickets Jerry Allison and Sonny Curtis recorded two old Holly tracks, 'That'll Be The Day' and 'It Doesn't Matter Anymore', as the framework for a proposed tribute to Holly.

Originally restricted by staff producers with fixed views on country, Jennings's early material was basically conventional *modern* country, highlighted only by his brilliant interpretation of lyrics — as on 'MacArthur Park' and 'Days Of Sand And Shovels' (both in 1966) — and his soulful voice.

Producers like Herb Alpert, Danny Davis and Chet Atkins did little to draw out Jennings's latent talent and it was possibly this stifling of creative development that caused the artist to 'buck' the system and eventually strike out on his own.

Following a successful but unremarkable period with RCA Victor, Jennings almost broke with the label over policy and only when they agreed to let him produce his own sessions were the foundations laid for his acceptance outside country music.

Along with Billy Joe Shaver and Tompall Glaser, Jennings had been called "one of the last real cowboys," but he was no range rider, rather a man fighting for the freedom of country music and striving to put back the individuality that Nashville had taken away over the years. Many country fans accused Jennings of veering away from country completely but that couldn't have been further from the truth.

Jet-Age Cowboy

As Roger Schutt, an American magazine and TV writer observed in his liner notes for Jennings's 'Honky Tonk Heroes' album: "It's more than just a possibility that the songs in this album will become the 'Cool Water' and 'Tumbling Tumbleweed' anthems of the jet-age cowboy."

The album, released in 1973, contained songs written by Billy Joe Shaver ('Honky Tonk Heroes', 'Old Five And Dimers', 'Willie The Wandering Gypsy And Me', 'Low Down Freedom', 'Ride Me Down Easy', 'Ain't No God In Mexico' and 'Black Rose'), Donnie Fritts and Troy Seals ('We Had It All') and co-productions by Shaver and Jennings ('You Ask Me To') and Shaver and Hillman Hall ('Omaha').

Another aspect of Jennings's early associations with RCA that encouraged him to fight for his principles was the reluctance of the company to let the Waylors (Jennings's road band) accompany him on recordings. When he became an independent entity so far as production was concerned, he augmented the usual back-up musicians like Joe Allen, Ralph Mooney, Hargus Robbins, David Briggs, Jimmy Capps and Charlie McCoy, with his own hard-driving, rock-based group.

Jennings's intention with the 'Honky Tonk Heroes' album was to create a new style of cowboy songs and it was a recurring theme throughout his recordings. They weren't 'western' cowboy songs in the true sense but ballads laying down his beliefs, odes to close friends ('Willie The Wandering Gypsy' was written about Willie Nelson, another Nashville "outlaw"), and gentle love songs. His own songwriting output was prolific and over the years Jennings wrote some beautiful material in the shape of 'Anita, You're Dreaming' and 'Just To Satisfy You' (both written in conjunction with Don Bowman), 'Sure Didn't Take Him Long' and 'I Think It's Time She Learned' (written with Miriam Eddy), 'This Time' and 'Rainy Day Woman'.

A close study of his recorded material, however, shows that Waylon Jennings was anxious to take in as broad a spectrum of

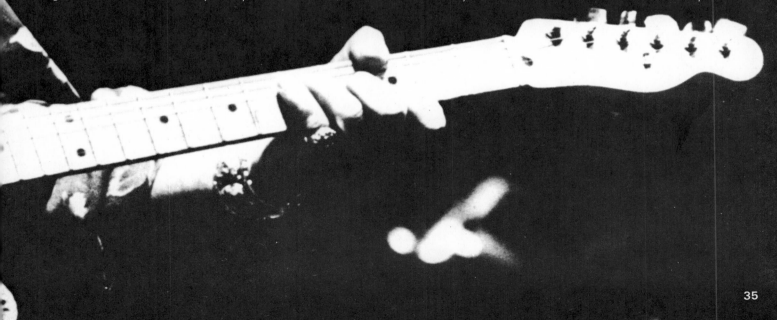

contemporary music as possible and not restrict himself to the close confines of country. Among the composers he drew upon over the years were Jim Webb, Chuck Berry, Paul Simon, Neil Diamond, Johnny Cash, Kris Kristofferson, J. J. Cale, Gregg Allman, Bob Dylan, Lennon and McCartney and even Bill Martin and Phil Coulter.

The vast changes in Jennings's attitudes to his music are reflected through his various sleeve photographs. Until his almost revolutionary 'Ladies Love Outlaws' album, produced by Ronnie Light in 1972, Jennings was almost staid in appearance but then the cowboy, struggling for so long to be accepted, burst through and a new image presented itself. The sideburns and hair grew longer and unkempt, and the frock coats were replaced by faded jeans and leather boots. Jennings had rid himself of the Nashville shackles and he wasn't afraid to voice his opinions to the world.

Solidly Country

"I'm a part of country music and that's where it's at," he commented. "I say what I say and I do what I do because I love the music and sometimes I feel there are wrongs. I'm not out to change things. I may criticize at times but I'll be the first to defend country music and what it stands for."

Strangely enough, Jennings, while earning the respect of musicians and singers the world over, hadn't made a great impact outside America by the mid-'70s. His 1972

appearance at the International Festival of Country Music at Wembley, England, was marred by an inadequate sound system that did nothing to enhance his image. The organizers maintained that Jennings's performance — and that of his wife, Jessi Colter — was below standard and yet those close enough to the stage heard Jennings's vocal mike "breaking up."

He was philosophical about it and decided that even if the PA hadn't been faulty maybe he wasn't ready for British audiences at that particular time, but his albums released in Britain didn't measure up to the sales achieved by Johnny Cash, Marty Robbins or Charlie Pride. In America, however, Jennings was a giant and his albums were colossal successes.

His numerous appearances at the Troubadour in Los Angeles and the Bottom Line Club in New York, both noted rock venues, drew his music even closer to the pop field but in doing so it gave an even wider acceptance to *country* music. In spite of Jennings's close associations with rock musicians he had no intention of deserting country music. "I couldn't go pop with a mouthful of firecrackers," he said, "and whatever I do will be solidly country."

In his native Texas he was a disc jockey and occasional performer, appearing in talent shows and clubs both in Texas and Arizona. In 1966 he left Texas for Nashville, Tennessee, and signed with RCA under the direction of Chet Atkins. The same year he appeared in a low-budget Nashville movie appropriately titled *The*

Nashville Rebel, but it took another seven years for his career to flourish and to make any marked impression on the city.

Jennings was a modern cowboy without a horse, a rebel with a cause, and was joined by other Nashville system-kickers. Kris Kristofferson, Billy Joe Shaver, Willie Nelson, Jerry Jeff Walker, Tompall Glaser and, to some degree, Tom T. Hall all had a new message to spread and their claim grew too big and successful to ignore.

Outlaw Clan

Nashville begrudgingly accepted their presence and admitted that the 'rebels' had something tangible to offer country music. Jennings and Kristofferson gave country music something it had always lacked — sex appeal — while the remaining 'outlaw' members injected 'Music City, USA' with a new style of country music performer.

As a performer, Jennings was the most popular of America's '70s 'outlaw' clan and his appeal stretched to one of the most unlikely sections of America's community, the Navajo Indians of New Mexico. The Indians liked Jennings and they respected his music. Each year on December 31, Jennings performed for them at the Catholic Indian Centre in Gallup and the tribe adopted the singer's old hit, 'Love Of The Common People', as their unofficial anthem.

Success to Jennings didn't simply mean financial reward, success was putting something vital back into country music and coming to terms with the establishment. Nashville was taking the country out of country music but Jennings, with his searing, soul-rending voice, let people know that country was *their* music.

His ambition in the mid-'70s seemed to be in the direction of rock & roll from the days when Buddy Holly and the Crickets were recording songs like 'Brown-Eyed Handsome Man', 'Peggy Sue' and 'Everyday'. He is quoted as saying: "I'm going to let my music take me wherever I go. Instruments don't make country. We're entitled to a heavy rock beat if it complements our songs. Why should we lock ourselves in?"

For all his cult successes Jennings was modest to the point of even putting down his own guitar playing. "Hell, I ain't no great guitar player," he admitted. "I just play my stuff. I'm very self-conscious about my guitar playing for some reason. I'm a singer, I never practise on my guitar."

In the mid-'60s Jennings was a hell-raiser, and stories of his wrecking exploits with Johnny Cash, with whom he shared a bachelor pad, were legion. Later the violence was replaced by a constructive rebellion aimed at doing what he felt was right for American country music.

If anyone told him that they didn't dig the kind of country music he was into, he was likely to tell them to go to hell, but secretly he hoped they were into his particular scene and it really bothered him to think that he wasn't getting the message across.

Below: Waylon Jennings (on the right) in concert with his country music band.

John Denver

When Henry John Deutchendorf got his first recording contract he decided that his name wouldn't look exactly right on a record label. So he changed it — to John Denver.

Born early on in the post-war 'baby boom', John and his younger brother, Ronald, grew up in a US Air Force family, and received their education in a succession of schools between Florida and Japan. Their father was a pilot, holding three world records in military aviation, and for a time John had such ambitions too, until he got turned on to music. This happened at an early age, when his grandmother gave him an old 1910 Gibson guitar on which he began practising, and eventually John became adept on both the 6 and the 12-string versions.

His initial interest in music was the rock & roll of Elvis Presley but, when he went to college in Texas to study architecture, this interest quickly changed to an involvement in the folk music scene that was being spearheaded by Bob Dylan. From Texas, Denver felt compelled to move to the West Coast to try his luck in show-business. He played a number of small spots and then auditioned at Leadbetter's in Los Angeles, where he was hired by folk impresario Randy Sparks. Then, when Chad Mitchell

split from the trio bearing his name, Denver won out over 250 other applicants for the vacancy. He stayed with the trio for nearly four years before striking out on his own.

The record that set him on the road to stardom was 'Rhymes And Reasons' which included the famous 'Leaving On A Jet Plane', a million-seller for Peter, Paul and Mary in 1969. Since then the song has been recorded by, among others, Spanky and Our Gang, Eddy Arnold, Floyd Cramer, Bob Carlin, and Liza Minelli, and has become almost a folk-rock standard.

Released in 1969 in the States, 'Rhymes And Reasons' contained 14 tracks, although only four were Denver's own compositions: 'Daydream', 'Circus', 'Rhymes And Reasons', and, of course, 'Leaving On A Jet Plane'. Among the other writers represented on this set were Lennon and McCartney, with 'When I'm 64', and Tom Paxton. With the compositions of Tom Paxton, John really laid his political thoughts on the line, for the numbers he chose were both facetious pieces about Spiro Agnew and Richard Nixon. On later albums, John was to use further Paxton songs, and also became a frequent user of the Lennon and McCartney songbook — producing notable interpretations of 'Eleanor Rigby', 'Let It Be' and 'Mother Nature's Son'.

'Rhymes And Reasons' was both sad

and reflective *and* gentle and light, and Denver sang this collection of straightforward, unpretentious songs in a clear, controlled manner — thereby revealing what was to be expected from him in the future in both subject-matter and style. His use of other people's material was also to continue and in November, 1972, he perhaps explained why when he spoke about his voice and his songwriting to the *Manhattan State Collegian*: ''I'm not a great singer like Harry Nilsson, and I know I'm not a great songwriter like Kristofferson or Dylan. I'm hardly what you would call prolific.

''I really have a hard time writing songs. If I can write one a month I feel good. 'Poems, Prayers And Promises' took six months. But I do think I'm a very good performer, and that's where it's at for me.''

'Rhymes And Reasons' was a successful record, and was followed by 'Take Me To Tomorrow', a heavier album that contained six songs penned by Denver, as well as some by Tom Paxton, Jacques Brel and Biff Taylor.

'Whose Garden Was This', this time with a Paxton number as title track, was Denver's third US album release, but it was 'Poems, Prayers And Promises' that really established him as a prospective chart regular in the States. The album quickly went Gold, and was followed

SKR

successfully by all the later Denver albums.

Kris Kristofferson's 'Casey's Last Ride', John Prine's 'Blow Up Your TV', and Buddy Holly's 'Everyday' were all included on 'Aerie', the fifth Denver album, although his own 'Starwood In Aspen' was probably the record's supreme track.

The real landmark in John Denver's recording career, though, came with his sixth album, 'Rocky Mountain High'. Not only did this record sell a lot more than its predecessors — it was awarded a platinum record in the States for selling over 1,000,000 (a Gold Disc merely represents sales of over $1,000,000) — but it also attracted almost as much critical acclaim as all the earlier albums put together. It was described as 'a crisp, muscular album with compelling singing and some of the most powerful acoustic guitar-dominated arrangements heard on record.' As an added bonus, the title track, which was released as a single, also achieved Gold Disc status.

After that, the next album, 'Farewell Andromeda', could hardly have failed, and it quickly racked up another $1,000,000 sales figure for John. Despite his huge success with the record-buying public however, John Denver remained the subject of much critical sniping on both sides of the Atlantic. This scepticism was to a degree inevitable by 1974, for singer/songwriters were no longer as fashionable as they were at the peak of James Taylor's success in 1972.

In his sell-out concerts at New York's Madison Square Garden and Carnegie Hall, his frequent TV appearances, his all-American Boy image — he frequently performed 'America The Beautiful' on stage — all seem at odds with the sentiments he so often expressed on record. John often appeared to be the singer/songwriter for suburban Middle America.

One reviewer dwelt on the negative aspects of Denver:

"There he is on the screen of your colour TV: blond, bespectacled, and peach-faced — the sight of him makes you want to adjust the hue, because John Denver's flesh tone is just a shade too flesh-toned. He's the balladeer for the masses, sweet-voiced, ingenuous, and completely devoid of human characteristics. He seems sincere enough, but it's hard to sense any character in anything he says or sings."

Ecological Concern

It *is* possible that John Denver jumped on the ecology bandwagon, and yet it is equally possible that his was a voice of genuine concern. If he is to be taken as being genuinely sincere, then several of his later lyrics become more credible and more palatable:

Welcome to my morning, welcome to my day
Oh yes, I'm the one responsible
I made it just this way
To take myself some pictures and see what they might bring

These lyrics, from 'Farewell Andromeda',

John Denver, all-American country boy.

are much more compatible with John's saying that "music is not so much a form of entertainment as a life-style of people, like those who came together at Woodstock." In fact Denver often spoke of his relationship with his audience: "I'm not in this business to make a killing, not in this business to be the biggest entertainer in the world. I like to sing for people. I think that's what I am, more than a songwriter or recording artist. I'm an entertainer." John Denver, in other words, wants "to be friends with people" and explained how he uses the concert hall to express his beliefs: "I don't think I'm an activist to the extent of going out there and campaigning for a bunch of things on my own. I have certain feelings and it would be impossible for me to hide those in the shows I do."

Perhaps the best expression of how Denver attempts to communicate with his audiences comes when he says that he "doesn't want to entertain people . . . I want to touch them."

His feelings about the beauty of the world and of its possible destruction by progress come across when he tells an audience that: "The one thing that we have today is this country of ours, this beautiful planet, Mother Earth." Or when he reportedly said: "I love being up onstage and singing to people, even more than living in the Rocky Mountains, because onstage I can go back to the Rockies and take people with me."

In January, 1973, John Denver received ecstatic reviews from the American press after the showing of an ecology-orientated TV special, *Big Horn*. There was, however, a certain irony in that the show's sponsors were General Electric. Although the programme was a documentary — on the subject of Rocky Mountain sheep — it is possible that it was one of the main reasons behind

the BBC's rather puzzling decision to invite Denver to London to star in his own TV series, *The John Denver Show*. At the time, John was somewhat bemused by it all. He had won tumultuous applause at London's Empire Pool when he played as support act to the Moody Blues in the Spring of 1972; he had made a successful star appearance on a TV series called *They Sold A Million*; and yet he still wasn't entirely sure why he had been invited to London to make the programmes because, in his own words, "I've had no record success in England, I mean none."

The Sunday night TV show, however, certainly changed that. Although Olivia Newton-John had scored in the British charts with his no.1 US hit, 'Take Me Home Country Roads', Denver's own records had had no tangible success at all — in fact his first three albums had never even been released. So vastly did his popularity rise in Britain, however, after the first broadcasts, that RCA had to rush out copies of 'Rhymes And Reasons', 'Take Me To Tomorrow' and 'Whose Garden Was This' to keep up with the demand for his records.

By the end of 1973 then, John Denver had become one of the most consistent album sellers on both sides of the Atlantic, and for his British audience particularly, he seemed to have acquired the aura of something like a sanitized Bob Dylan. Criticism of his image from the serious music critics nevertheless continued unabated — in fact from the first programme of his BBC series, critical opinion seemed to be in inverse ratio to audience reaction. Denver, though, seemed to have his future pretty well tied up as he continually diversified his appeal — one day he would be guest-hosting America's *Tonight Show* and attempting to pour life into Mark Spitz, and another day he would be heard to have taken legal action against a land developer who'd been dubbing 'Rocky Mountain High' onto his TV commercials.

John was a seeming walking contradiction — a *concerned* all-American Boy. He liked sports and playing around on motorbikes and, of course, he drank a lot of milk. Yet then he'd go out and get uptight about ecology, Vietnam, or social injustices. Milt Okun, his producer, attempted to explain away this contradiction: "To be or not to be is hardly the question for John. He already is."

By 1974 Denver looked as if set to be the first Perry Como of the rock & roll business — hosting his own weekly song and dance TV show until he either tired of it or his ratings began to slip. But John Denver was already prepared for the fact that he must come to the end of his success run sometime.

"Some day," he said, "people will come up and say 'It's all over. You're passé'. And I'll say 'Beautiful'. And I'll go back to the Rocky Mountains and I'll raise a family. Annie (his wife) and I want to have a little restaurant. She'll cook and I'll wait on tables and sing.

"And I'll find no less joy there than in what I'm doing now."

Charlie Rich: The Silver Fox

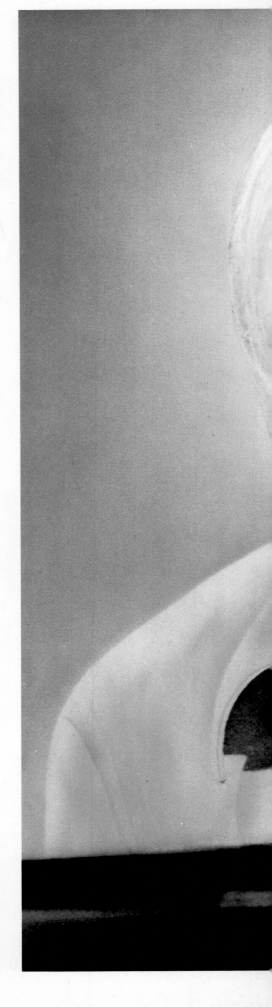

Charlie Rich was one of the few people who successfully established themselves in two fields of music. Until the '70s he was associated solely with the Sun recording era and the rockabilly boom of the '50s, but then became recognized as a country star.

Born in Colt, Arkansas, on December 14, 1934, Rich spent his formative years listening to jazz bands and religious music and to a large degree his easy-flowing vocal style throughout his career retained elements of those younger days.

Rich became a saxophonist in his high school band and also learned to play piano. Much of his experience was gained from working with small jazz and blues combos and an intensive study of the roots of the music left an almost indelible characteristic jazz feel on his singing.

In 1952 Rich entered the University of Arkansas, where he studied musical theory and just over a year later enlisted in the air force and was posted to Oklahoma, where he formed his first jazz band, the Velvetones, and gained a regular spot on a local TV station. Rich played mostly piano and sax in those days, preferring to leave any vocals to his wife, Margaret. Upon discharge he broke up the Velvetones and moved to West Memphis, working on his father's cotton plantation and jamming with local jazz bands.

Jerry Lee Lewis

He began session work for the Judd label, a company owned by Judd Phillips, brother of Sun's Sam Phillips, and Judd, suitably impressed with Rich's style, brought him to the attention of producer Bill Justis. Rich discussed material with Justis (who recorded the rock classic 'Raunchy' in 1958) and a session for Sun was arranged. According to Justis, however, Rich was far too jazzy in his approach and was advised to study the recordings of Jerry Lee Lewis.

"I told him to come back when he could get that bad!" Justis recalled. "His voice was fine but his songs and musical arrangements were far too complicated."

Sun was taking basic rock & roll and giving it an up-tempo hillbilly treatment, resulting in a musical hybrid later to be called rockabilly. Simplicity was what Phillips was after and in Rich he saw more than was at first apparent.

Charlie did as Justis suggested and made an intensive study of Jerry Lee's records, and recordings by other up-and-coming artists on the label. Eventually he adjusted his phrasing and smoothed out his jazz intonations, the result being a fusion of all that Rich had gleaned from fellow musicians.

Orthodox Country Boys

At that time Memphis was a hotbed of creative activity, with hundreds of one-shot record labels springing up with a view to cashing in on the new boom. It was the spawning ground for Johnny Cash, Warren Smith, Luke McDaniel, Jerry Lee Lewis, Carl Perkins and Roy Orbison and, once the chart successes began to emerge, innumerable orthodox country boys from the hills began flooding into the city in an attempt to save their careers from the merciless onslaught of rock & roll. The rock & roll emergence was almost the coup de grace for country music and the careers of those artists unable or unwilling to make the transition often suffered permanent damage.

Charlie Rich was one of the more fortunate 'unknown' artists associated with Memphis. Whereas several *name* country performers had striven to ride out the rock & roll boom by switching styles, ultimately failing and losing to both rock & roll audiences and their former fans, Rich was literally in at the beginning.

Rich finally signed with Phillips and the first session, resulting in 'Whirlwind', proved that Charlie had indeed listened intently to other Sun recordings, because the initial single was moulded in the style of Jerry Lee Lewis rockers for the same label. The single, however, was not a commercial success and the follow-up, 'Rebound', did little to rectify the situation. By this time Rich realized that he was not a rock & roll singer and he abandoned the style in favour of session work and songwriting. Johnny Cash had already been

successful with one Rich composition, 'The Ways Of A Woman In Love', and in his capacity as a writer Charlie eventually contributed many excellent songs to the middle-of-the-road country repertoire.

In 1959, however, the situation changed dramatically when Sun released Rich's own 'Lonely Weekends'. The Rich style had mellowed slightly and although the basic background still owed much to Jerry Lee Lewis, an individual vocal technique and unique beat took the record into the national charts. Whether Rich actually strove to create this individual beat is open to speculation but, while certain musical historians claim that it was a fusion of rock and jazz rhythms – both familiar to Rich – there was an over-riding *country* feel to the track that put Rich a few years ahead of his time.

The Setting Sun

'Lonely Weekends' went on to sell half a million and a few months later an album of that title was released and was considered by many to be one of the outstanding recordings of that period in pop-country history. The album gave Rich a broad canvas upon which to work and included jazz, pop, country and rock styles.

By 1962 it became evident that the great days of Sun were coming to an end and when Charlie's contract ended he spent a fairly successful two years with an RCA subsidiary label, Groove, under the guidance of Justis, who had been sacked from Sun Records shortly after Rich cut 'Whirlwind'.

Justis had a lot of faith in Rich and for a time the singer's career was quite successful with such singles as 'Big Boss Man', 'Ways Of A Woman In Love' and 'Lady Love' earning him a reputation as a consistent, if not spectacular, hitmaker. A subsequent middle-of-the-road country album, however, was not a success and it marked a low spot in Rich's otherwise stable career.

In 1965 Charlie signed with the Smash label and was promoted as a rock artist, resulting in a novelty hit, 'Mohair Sam', penned by the ubiquitous and highly respected Dallas Frazier. The accompanying album partially recalled Rich's brief excursion into the country field, but his now-pounding piano style was a marked feature. Two years later Rich's contract with Smash was terminated and he joined the smaller Hi label, but they mishandled him and for a time it seemed that his career was destined to crumble. Rich understandably left Hi and came to the attention of Epic who, in 1965, were developing a country catalogue. A contract was signed and Rich came under the expert guidance of Billy Sherrill.

For the first three years of his Epic contract Rich had little success, though many of the titles he recorded for Sherrill were excellent and included 'By The Time I Get To Phoenix', 'Raggedy

Left: Charlie Rich successfully crossed over from rock & roll to country music.

Ann' and 'I Almost Lost My Mind'. During this period Rich never achieved more than modest sales for his recordings, but Epic persisted with him.

Throughout 1971 Charlie 'rested' and no more Epic products of his were issued. Various re-issues from other sources did little to enhance his reputation and for a time it seemed unlikely that he would survive with Epic. Midway through the following year, however, they released 'I Take It On Home', written by an up-and-coming country writer, Kenny O'Dell, coupled with Rich's own 'Peace On You'. The single was an instant success in both pop and country fields and it later received a Grammy nomination.

Eager to capitalize on Rich's new-found chart success Epic compiled 'The Best Of Charlie Rich', with tracks taken from his first three albums for that label, 'Set Me Free', 'The Fabulous Charlie Rich' and 'Big Boss Man'. The new album proved to be one of the turning points in Rich's career and it became another cross-over best-seller. Shortly after this release Rich recorded another Kenny O'Dell song, the now historic 'Behind Closed Doors'. Rich became an 'overnight sensation' and, for the first time in his long career, maintained that success by recording a remarkable number of outstanding hits, including 'The Most Beautiful Girl', 'My Elusive Dreams' and 'She Called Me Baby'.

Rich Philosophy

Like so many other long-standing artists who develop into 'overnight sensations', Rich was philosophical about his fame. "The only way a white guy around 40 can make it in the business these days is to be classified as a 'country' singer, but basically I'm doing what I've always done," he said in reply to people's questions.

Others might not have agreed that Rich was "doing what he's always done" but a closer analysis of his earlier days with the Sun label revealed much activity in country music, ranging from straight session piano on recordings by Johnny Cash, Sonny Burgess and Carl Mann, to prolific songwriting.

In his book *Feel Like Going Home*, Peter Guralnick said of Rich: "He is a musician of extraordinary eclecticism, someone in whom a variety of musical elements have fused to create an artist who functions with all the necessity of a country or blues performer but with considerably greater complexity. He has a voice of remarkable range and feeling which he uses to great emotional effect. The material he does is very much his own personal brand of soul, encompassing almost the entire spectrum of American popular music."

Glen Campbell
Gentle On Your Mind

"What success I've had," Glen Campbell once said, "comes from going against the grain of contemporary performers. My hair isn't falling in my face and I don't play electronic, freaked-out music. I went through all that. There's nothing wrong with being American-looking and playing popular music. I copied from Dean Martin. He doesn't try too hard to sell people on his personality or his music. He just plays it nice and easy. Folks enjoy and appreciate that."

Campbell epitomized Hollywood's old image of the clean-cut, all-American boy, with his impeccable clothes, neatly-squared sideburns and infectious, almost boyish smile. Yet, for all his apparent untrendy wholesomeness, Campbell was no slouch musician, as many of his pop contemporaries will readily testify.

Born in Delight, Arkansas, in 1933, Glen Campbell grew up in a solid country music environment listening to the old ballads of his parents, Carrie and Wesley. His career, however, embraced many styles of music, and country played only a minor role in his ultimate development as an artist of international standing.

While still in his teens Glen moved from rural Arkansas to Albuquerque, New Mexico, where he joined his uncle, Dick Bill, in a small combo. Glen later formed his own band and held down a residency at a local night club for six years, before moving to Los Angeles to work as a session guitarist for Capitol Records.

Campbell's numerous sessions for Capitol called for him to play the guitar in a variety of styles, including jazz, rock and conventional country music, and among the artists he recorded with were Frank Sinatra, Jack Jones, the Mamas & Papas, Nat 'King' Cole, Dean Martin and Elvis Presley.

By this time Campbell had become a superior all-round musician, with a particular talent for the 12-string guitar and during his formative years cut some interesting tracks for World Pacific Records with an instrumental folk-country combo known as the Folkswingers. The songs Campbell cut with the group included 'Black Mountain Rag', 'East Virginia' and 'Gotta Travel On'. The feature of those tracks was Campbell's hard-driving and proficient 12-string guitar technique.

To supplement his income he divided his time between cutting vocal demo sessions for other local companies and playing with a studio band called the Champs. Other studio bands, like the Piltdown Men and later Area Code 615, achieved a fair measure of chart success and the Champs' contributions to pop history were 'Tequila' and 'Limbo Rock', both of which included Glen Campbell in the line-up.

A bona fide group, the Beach Boys, also made use of Campbell's diverse talents when Brian Wilson was hospitalized for a six-month period. Campbell was called in as a temporary replacement and, although he never actually recorded with the group, he did sing vocal harmonies on stage.

Urban-Folk Revival

While Campbell's main source of income in those early days came from session work and odd stints with multifarious groups, his country music background wasn't entirely dismissed. In 1962 he went into the Capitol Studios with Dale Fitzsimmons and Carl Tanberg, a duo known as the Green Briar Boys, and recorded 12 country tracks. The resulting album, 'Big Bluegrass Special', was obviously designed to catch the lucrative urban-folk revival market and, whereas the music — anything but authentic bluegrass — did little to slake the voracious appetites of the revivalists, Campbell's sterling vocal work on songs like 'Truck Driving Man', 'No Vacancy', 'Brown's Ferry Blues' and the now-classic 'Long Black Limousine' brought him to the attention of country music audiences in the US and the UK.

Campbell had tasted modest success with two previous pop-flavoured singles, 'Turn Around, Look At Me' and 'Too Late To Worry, Too Blue To Cry', but it was 'Big Bluegrass Special' that established him as a 'name to watch' in the national country music charts.

Eventually Capitol acknowledged the fact that Glen Campbell was more than just a good session musician who could turn in satisfactory country-oriented recordings from time to time and in 1967 they consolidated his initial chart success with 'Burning Bridges'. Pop-wise the single did nothing for Campbell's reputation and it wasn't until later that same year, when he recorded John Hartford's 'Gentle On My Mind', that his true potential was realized. In fact 1967 was a decisive year for Campbell for, in the wake of 'Burning Bridges' and 'Gentle On My Mind', came

Below: Glen Campbell with Anne ('Snowbird') Murray, another popularizer of country.

his first award-winning song, 'By The Time I Get To Phoenix', penned by Jim Webb. Campbell received a Grammy for the Best Solo Vocal Performance, a second Grammy for the Best Contemporary (R&R) Vocal Performance and another for the Album Of The Year (Popular).

Jim Webb and Glen Campbell formed a close friendship and two other massive cross-over hits (country and pop charts), 'Wichita Lineman' and 'Galveston', followed. Campbell maintained his chart status with 'Dreams Of The Everyday Housewife', 'Hey Little One' and 'I Wanna Live' before a fourth Jimmy Webb composition, 'Where's The Playground Susie', provided him with another substantial hit. By this time Webb was pursuing a solo career and the liaison ceased.

With so many hits behind him Campbell was firmly established in the pop field and his concert appearances were building him into a superstar. The pop world had accepted him but Campbell was quick to acknowledge his country music influences and eventually he introduced a young teenage banjo player, Carl Jackson, into his stage act — Jackson became a star in his own right and an integral part of *The Glen Campbell Show*.

In 1969 Capitol teamed Glen with Bobbie Gentry, a Southern singer who had scored resoundingly two years earlier with her own composition 'Ode To Billy Joe', and they took an old Everly Brothers hit, 'Let It Be Me', into the pop and country charts. The following year Glen and Bobbie teamed again for a second Everly Brothers revival, 'All I Have To Do Is Dream'. Campbell's solo career flourished and his subsequent hits included 'Dream Baby', '(London) I'm Coming To See You' and 'Bonaparte's Retreat'.

Throughout his entire career Campbell never recorded a *bad* song. ''I start with the story, and then it has to be easy to sing,'' he said. ''There are a lot of rock records but that's not what I do. Rock records are more or less beat records, I need a good melody, too. That was half the success of Jimmy Webb, what he does is marry a real good lyric with a more or less classic melody.''

Boy-Next-Door Good Looks

In between pop-slanted titles like 'Oh, Happy Day' and 'Bridge Over Troubled Water', Campbell returned to his country roots and recorded songs nearer to the soil of his rural home-state, songs like 'Bonaparte's Retreat', an old classic by Pee Wee King, and 'Lovesick Blues', once associated with Slim Whitman and the late Hank Williams which became as much Campbell's song as anyone else's — he had a way of taking a song and making it his own.

Campbell's boy-next-door good looks helped his musical career tremendously and in 1969 they led to his being cast in a starring role alongside John Wayne in Hal Wallis's award-winning western *True Grit*. The movie was excellent and Campbell turned in a commendable performance,

Left: Glen Campbell with the old-timer John Wayne in the movie *True Grit*.

but he was uneasy with close up cameras.

"Doin' a movie is slow," he told an interviewer. "I don't seem to be able to get anything going in a movie. *Norwood* (his second movie for Hal Wallis) was a drag because we were sitting in a trailer on a car going 30 miles an hour doin' nothin' for days while the camera was goin'." *Norwood* was a failure compared to *True Grit* and Campbell wasn't anxious to involve himself too heavily in the movie industry. "I much prefer working to *live* audiences," he said candidly.

Nevertheless, *True Grit* provided him with an alternative career and a further hit in the shape of the movie's theme song. Campbell was actually contracted to appear in three movies for Hal Wallis but following the comparative commercial failure of the folksy-flavoured *Norwood*, he was reluctant to jeopardize his image as a singer.

Mastering The Bagpipes

Like most Americans, Glen Campbell was proud of his ancestry and having traced his family tree back to Scotland, Glen spent months mastering the bagpipes, which he featured in his stage act. Carrie and Wesley Campbell were also a feature of their son's act and from time to time he introduced them to perform at least two old-time country numbers.

Campbell's music became a little hard to define and he refused to be labelled 'country' or otherwise. It's significant to note that many of his later hits figured in the country music charts, as well as registering in the pop field. His appeal was wide and a typical concert appearance included an amazingly wide repertoire, ranging from the songs of Jim Webb, Ralph McTell, Charles Aznavour and Rodgers and Hammerstein, to country-rooted material. In later years the country music content of Campbell's record and stage repertoire was extended to include bluegrass.

In Britain Campbell was extremely successful and his regular concert tours were sell-outs. Ember Records acquired a number of the artist's albums for UK distribution in the days when Campbell was more country-oriented and Capitol weren't convinced of his appeal outside the United States. Jeff Kruger, who headed the Ember label and a subsidiary concert division, saw the potential in Glen Campbell and successfully promoted him as a middle-of-the-road performer.

From an initial charity concert, followed by an exploratory tour of selected venues in Britain, Glen rose to become as big in the UK as he was in America. His rise to fame wasn't meteoric but each stage in his career was significant. Campbell knew what he wanted but he also knew that success doesn't necessarily come easy. "I know what I want to do, but it's damn hard to do it," he said with a degree of seriousness.

KRIS
KRISTOFFERSON

Nashville, as much as any other big music centre in the world, has been through many changes since rock & roll first set the ball rolling in the mid-'50s. In the process, it undoubtedly widened its once restricted and anti-liberal horizons.

Still the traditional centre for country music in the States, it at last threw open its doors to countless rock musicians who recorded there. But this was meeting the outside world half-way, and more important the new attitudes being bred in the city itself.

Even before country music began reaching out to grab the attention of rock audiences, Nashville was preparing itself to meet this new challenge. It was to this gradually evolving Nashville — a city ready for new possibilities and new talent — that a young, if not too young, ex-army helicopter pilot and Rhodes scholar came to settle, to try his hand at songwriting. And Nashville was ready for him. Kris Kristofferson chanced his luck and succeeded.

Kris Kristofferson was born in Brownsville, Texas, in June 1936, and lived there until he went to high school. At that time country music wasn't as popular as it later became, but Kris was listening to the local radio stations beaming out country, and buying Hank Williams records even if he was thought a little strange and out of time for doing so.

Kris's family kept on the move, taking in San Mateo, California, Virginia, Florida, returning to Texas and then back to California again about the time he was ready to go to college. It's not surprising to find this rootless meandering reflected in the content and easy-going style of his songs.

Once in California again, Kris decided to stay even though his family moved on. He attended the small liberal arts college of Pomono in the southern part of the state. Then, his talents were free to expand in perhaps surprising directions for the denim clad, rough-shod cowboy he came to represent. Back then, he excelled as a Golden Gloves boxer, a football player, sports writer and Reserve Officer Training Corps (ROTC) Commander. But, looking ahead to his future career, Pomono saw two very significant areas of his future

Kris Kristofferson on guitar and Rita Coolidge, the '70s Sonny and Cher of rock.

development. One was as a creative writer, the other as a reasonable folk singer. As a writer he didn't quite turn out to be the next Scott Fitzgerald, although he did win several honours in an inter-college short-story competition. However, these diverse activities were enough to win him a Rhodes scholarship to Oxford on graduation in June 1958. While at Oxford, Kris kept on writing and completed a second novel. Both this and his first one were subsequently rejected by book publishers, but undaunted, he turned to his other love — writing songs. Kris was signed up by Tommy Steele's then manager, and became Kris Carson — 'the Yank at Oxford'. As he once said himself: "at that time I couldn't sing my way out of a paper bag." His first taste of the music business was soured by business hassles however, and thankfully he escaped from it in time. But the many academic years were beginning to produce a reaction. He received his Masters degree,

but left his doctorate within a year. Then it was back to the States to take up his ROTC commission and join the army, eventually extending his original two-year active duty spell to four and a half years.

This additional portion was, improbably, spent as a helicopter pilot in Germany, but the army stint wasn't perhaps so surprising if you consider that Kris's father was a retired Air Force Major General, and it had always been expected that he would follow a military career. So far everything was very much according to design. Kris was by now married with one child and another on the way. Everything was arranged for him to accept another assignment, along with promotion from Captain to Major to teach English at West Point Military Academy.

Underneath all this, the creative writer was still there waiting to be released, but this side of his life was becoming more and more repressed. Kris had always led his

Above: Kris Kristofferson and Susan Anspach starring in the movie, *Blume In Love,* a funny-sad love story written, produced and directed by Paul Mazursky. Right: Kris Kristofferson playing Billy the Kid in the film *Pat Garrett And Billy The Kid.* With a cast that included such notables as James Coburn, Bob Dylan and Kris's wife, Rita Coolidge, Kris excelled himself and assured a safe career starring in movies in the future.

own life, yet here he was about to step into the ready-made US Army hierarchical structure. The conflict brought on a depression that drove him to extremes – apparently volunteering to go to Vietnam – but he was turned down and offered the softer option at West Point. He checked out West Point, but didn't care for it, and this more or less decided him to leave the service. What clinched it all was a shattering visit to Nashville. Another helicopter flier told him to look up a relative there, music publisher Marijohn Wilkins (she wrote 'Long Black Veil'), who introduced him to people with whom he had an opportunity to play and sing, even though he was only on leave for two weeks.

Nashville Landmark

In 1965 he left the army for good, and moved to Nashville . . . and never looked back. In retrospect, the day he arrived there must be marked as a landmark to the day progressive country came to Nashville.

Despite this, for Kris it had been a hard climb. To say the least, leaving the army to become a songwriter hadn't gone down well with his family, and it had caused a lot of bitterness. He moved to the city three months ahead of his wife, but the insecure life he had chosen was hardly the assured future of a West Point training officer, and before long the marriage broke up under the strain. The emotional upheaval of this time, which cut Kris off from his home, and then from his wife and children, was a painful experience and one which is indelibly engraved in the lines of many of his songs, notably one particular trauma from his 'Borderlord' album, on 'Burden Of Freedom':

Voices behind me still bitterly damn me
For seeking salvation they don't
understand

At this time, emotional survival was linked closely to financial survival, and Kris got by on money earned through a variety of jobs – construction work in a studio, studio set-up man, janitor, bartender ("Sixty dollars and all the beer I could drink"), to flying helicopters transporting men and equipment to offshore oil rigs in the Gulf of Mexico – as well as songwriting. The future looked grim, with legal fees from his divorce and medical fees from the birth of his second child, and when he wasn't commuting to the Gulf of Mexico he was slumming in a Nashville tenement. But as a songwriter he was beginning to be noticed. One couple especially helped him through this period, Johnny Cash and June Carter. Cash, who himself had been through hard times, could understand what it was like, and the two soon became good friends.

The first real break came when Roy Drusky recorded Kris's 'Jody And The Kid'. The record wasn't a hit, but it focused more attention on him from the likes of Jerry Kennedy and Fred Foster, former President of Monument Records. So, early in 1969,

Kris signed with the publishing arm of Foster's label and began hanging around the Johnny Cash show, showing people his material. Ray Stevens took 'Sunday Morning Coming Down', the song Johnny Cash later hit with, and others, like Gordon Lightfoot, became interested. Then Roger Miller – whom Kris had known for some time – found out he was a songwriter and persuaded Kris to play him a few songs and wound up recording three, including 'Me And Bobby McGee'.

The advance from these sales helped pay a few bills and freed Kris of the need to take another day job. By now he was starting to cut his own demos – Fred Foster kept his faith in him, and persuaded him to do an album for Monument. Far from feeling intimidated by the excellence of the Nashville cats who backed him, Kris was rapidly gaining confidence in himself as a performer, though not even his most devoted fans could claim he had a good singing voice. Even years later his coarse delivery remains unique, and on that first album (now titled 'Me And Bobby McGee') he sings out of tune a lot of the time, in a well-weathered monotone.

But a tour designed to smooth off the rough edges was being lined up. Fred Foster was still convinced his gamble with Kris would pay off and put up the expenses for the tour. He went on the road with a bunch of local musicians calling themselves the Band Of Thieves. Their debut was the Newport Folk Festival, then a spell in Greenwich Village was followed in the summer by appearances at the Big Sur Folk Festival and the Berkeley Folk Festival. When he returned to Nashville, Kris had garnered a firm following, and wasn't long in starting work on a new album. That album, 'The Silver Tongued Devil And I', displayed even more of a consistent writing talent than the first; besides a marked improvement in the vocal style, and an all-round good studio performance.

A Growing Reputation

His first two albums were rich in classic songs like 'Sunday Morning Coming Down', 'Help Me Make It Through The Night', 'The Taker' and the ubiquitous 'Me And Bobby McGee', with which Kris won the Country Music Association songwriter's award, a feat he later repeated. His reputation deservedly continued to grow. Built on his ability with words and his strong stage presence, he was able to maintain his high standards on two later albums, 'Borderlord' and 'Jesus Was A Capricorn', each one better than the last in terms of music.

In the meantime, more possibilities and opportunities were presenting themselves in the movie world, and Kris made appearances in *The Last Movie,* and *Cisco Pike.* He capped this, however, with leading roles in *Blume In Love* and *Pat Garrett And Billy The Kid. Billy The Kid* did for his movie career what Bobby McGee had done for his songwriting. In the movie Kris played the Kid in the same spontaneous and natural way that he sings, and as a result

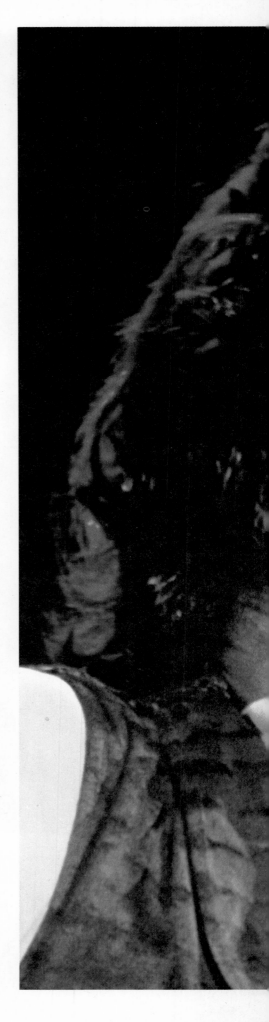

he seemed to guarantee himself a future in films. He married again, to Rita Coolidge. It was in 1972 when he first introduced Rita on stage — with a wry smile and an appropriate ''things'll be better now, we're bringing out somebody who can sing'' — and they went from sharing gigs, to sharing the stage, to sharing each other's lives. As performers their voices complemented each other beautifully, though they were far from matched as soloists. Rita appeared on two of Kris's albums — while he helped out on one song of 'The Lady's Not For Sale' — and they also cut a whole album together for A & M, entitled 'Full Moon'. 'Full Moon', surprisingly, was a somewhat disappointing album, and posed one or two questions for the future. While ranking alongside the 'Jesus Was A Capricorn' album in terms of the overall full sound quality, the distressing thing about it was the sparsity of Kristofferson originals — only two, plus two with Rita. In other words, it remained to be seen how his new stability would affect his songwriting. Where his previous material was built on themes of whiskey-soaked and beer-sodden despair, broken love affairs, some social comment and the sort of mapping experiences that can tear people up with their starkness, on 'Jesus Was A Capricorn' these themes were toned down considerably, with even the appearance of a couple of religious songs, 'Help Me' and 'Why Me'. The latter even won the 'Gospel Song of the Year' award, as well as being a top country hit. Kris reached the dilemma that, after years of almost being starved out of Nashville, he finally made it and seemed to be falling into the regular pattern for artists and groups during their transition to success. The hard edge was lost from his material, and his creativity was perhaps falling.

Nonetheless, even though Kristofferson may have been passing through this phase, there was already a second and third generation of contemporary country musicians following on in the Kristofferson mould — Billy Joe Shaver, Danny Epps, Guy Clark and Lee Clayton. All these new faces, together with the 'old school', came together in March 1972 for the Dripping Springs Reunion held in Texas, with Kris closing the show. The event was revived on July 4th, 1973 — this time as a rock festival with country entertainment . . . a change which signified the era Kris held open the doors for.

From the first, Kris was late in his arrival in the music business proper. He was already approaching 30 when he moved to Nashville, while other musicians such as Merle Haggard and Waylon Jenning already had a head start, although born about the same time. ''In terms of experience,'' Kris has remarked, ''Merle Haggard could be writing his own *Grapes Of Wrath* by now, particularly with several years of San Quentin behind him.'' Nonetheless, Kris's own entry into country music came at just the right time. Much earlier and neither the Nashville die-hards nor the rock enthusiasts, both equally hidebound in their own way, would have accepted him. As it is he found a firm following in both camps.

53

Olivia Newton-John

Olivia Newton-John — daughter of a Cambridge University professor was raised in Australia, rose to fame in Britain with her super-sweet singing and open-air good looks and went on to achieve success in the US's pop and country music fields.

'Livvy' (as she was widely known) sang with verve and appeal. She also had the sort of looks which could be expected to launch a career for her overnight, but the girl had her setbacks for all that — not the least being her involvement with an Anglo-American group, Toomorrow, which hit an all-time high in hypeing and flopped badly.

Olivia was born on September 26, 1948, the youngest of three children, her Welsh father being head of King's College, Cambridge. Her German-born mother was a daughter of scientist Max Born — one of the team which had split the atom, and a Nobel Prize winner. Five years later, Mr. Newton-John — a languages professor — accepted a college headship in Melbourne.

At 12, she won a cinema contest to find the girl who most looked like Hayley Mills and made her acting bow in *Green Pastures* in a Melbourne theatre.

"The first music to make an impression on me," said Olivia, "was country & western. I was forever dressing in western-style clothes, which I thought very romantic. When I was 14 I formed a singing group with three other girls. We called ourselves the Sol

Four and wore jeans, hessian jackets and desert boots, then our parents decided our studies were suffering and we had to disband. But I acted in school plays and felt I would one day make a go of it in show business. The only other career which appealed to me was as a vet."

Having caught up with her studies, she gained experience as a solo singer in a local coffee bar — it helped that the owner was married to her sister. Her first break came when she won a talent contest run by TV personality Johnny O'Keefe, the prize being a round trip to Britain, but her parents insisted she complete her studies first.

"My parents wanted me to go to university," she recalled. "My sister had opted out of this in favour of drama studies, and there was a bit of haggling when I said I also wanted to opt out and concentrate on singing, but my parents agreed when they realized how determined I was."

Olivia travelled to London with her mother, auditioned successfully for Decca a few weeks later and they released her first disc 'Till You Say You'll Be Mine' (written by Jackie de Shannon) in May, 1966. Her spell with Decca was short and uneventful, and when Pat Carroll, who had been another up-and-coming girl singer in Australia, arrived in London, they teamed up.

The Right Chemistry

As Pat and Olivia they played clubs, had spots on BBC TV, and did a show at Bournemouth that triggered off a chain of events vital to Olivia's future. She found herself talking to a man fixing some sound gear backstage whom she thought was a roadie. In fact he was Bruce Welch of the Shadows, who were doing a show there.

Though she and Bruce became friends, they parted company five weeks later, because Pat's work permit had lapsed, and Olivia went back to Australia with her. She was given her own TV series back home, but the following year she returned to Britain. Her friendship with Bruce Welch resumed and a few months later they became engaged.

She was sidetracked however from her solo plans when asked to join Toomorrow, which was masterminded by James Bond film producer Harry Saltzman and Don Kirschner — the disc producer who had created bubblegum groups the Monkees and the Archies. Toomorrow were to feature in a major movie and be launched on record and neither effort nor money was spared in an attempt to get the chemistry right.

Her partners in Toomorrow were Americans Ben Thomas and Karl Chambers and Britain's Vic Cooper. Toomorrow began work on their film late in 1969 and in 1970, the hypeing started. As the hand-outs said: "Livvy has buttery skin; big, big, very round; grey-green eyes; stands 5ft. 6ins. and weighs 98 lbs." She dug, they added, "Baez, horse riding, Mac Davis, Redford, Bruce Welch, McQueen, Streisand,

Feliciano, steak and salad, Hank Marvin, Beatles, wine, Bacharach and her Red Setter named Geordie."

Despite the Kirschner/Saltzman know-how and being on the RCA label, Toomorrow's first disc, 'You're My Baby Now', flopped badly. So too, despite all the lavish and dogged hypeing, did the film and their further chart bids, and soon after Toomorrow had finally become yesterday Olivia reverted to a solo career.

Through Bruce Welch, she had become friendly with the other Shadows (whose John Farrar had married Pat Carroll) and Cliff Richard. Recognizing her promise, he duetted with her on the B side of one of his discs — the first time he'd let a girl do that. He also featured her in his TV series and booked her for his Continental tour in the spring of 1971.

But even before the tour had begun, she had made it as a solo disc performer. Her first release on the Pye-released Festival label was Dylan's 'If Not For You', and despite competition from the great man himself, she beat him in the British charts. Her disc also scored in the US.

Though her next disc flopped, she cut her first solo album with Bruce Welch and John Farrar as producers, and included 'Banks Of The Ohio' — a Joan Baez favourite she had loved years before which late in 1971 as a single sold over a quarter of a million. Earlier that year she had topped a music paper poll; she repeated the feat early in 1972 and had another hit with 'What Is Life?' That April, her personal life made headlines when she and Bruce Welch ended their engagement and three days later he was rushed to hospital — reportedly because of a drugs overdose.

Her career continued to flourish in Britain and she scored another hit early in 1973 with 'Take Me Home, Country Roads'. In Britain that summer she flopped with 'Let Me Be There' by the late John Rostill of the Shadows, but the disc brought her her first Top Ten hit in the States and later won a Grammy award.

Top Country Song

She was performing in Australia in November when she had a phone call asking her to sing for Britain in the prestigious 1974 Eurovision Contest. Britain's song for the contest (held at Brighton, Sussex, in April, 1974) was 'Long Live Love' by Valerie Avon and Harold Spiro which came third, and Olivia was later quoted as saying she hadn't thought the song (picked by a viewers' vote) right for the event. But her record of it was a hit. Shortly after, however, she switched to EMI Records.

She went to the US for college dates and other gigs which included appearing at Disneyland and on the *Johnny Carson Show*. Her visit boosted her disc sales powerfully and 'If You Love Me, Let Me Know' became a Stateside hit. Her previous US hit, 'Let Me Be There', had

Right: Olivia's musical appeal has brought yet another country-pop fusion.

been voted top country song and it was in that field that much of her popularity was being established.

On a visit back to Britain in July, she said: "I'm in a fortunate position in the States. I'm considered a country cross-over act, which means I'm accepted by both country and pop. It's fantastic! Once country people accept you, they keep playing and buying your records."

She also declared: "In Tennessee they told me that unless you're born and bred in Nashville, it's usually impossible to be accepted as a country artist and that I should realize how lucky I was. Country fans are much more loyal than pop fans."

Olivia quickly followed her 'If You Love Me' success with an American no. 1 in 'I Honestly Love You' — right out of the country bracket and into pop — taped six TV shows with Andy Williams — realizing a girlhood dream by duetting with him. In October, 1974, she was named top girl singer by the Country Music Association.

In March, 1975, 'I Honestly Love You' won a Grammy as record of the year and the same disc brought her a second award for best vocal performance by a woman. At the time, her 'Have You Never Been Mellow?' was a hit in the US and she played to sell-out audiences there. That she might settle in the US seemed likely not only because of her thriving career there but because of a strong liaison with US showbiz executive Lee Kramer, whom she had met on a yacht in the South of France in 1973.

"Lee is my manager and boy friend," declared Olivia in April, 1975. "We've no immediate plans for marriage, but who knows?" (Her career had previously been guided by Peter Gormley — who had made his name as manager of Cliff Richard, the Shadows and other top artists.)

She returned to Britain in May, 1975, after having been in the States for the previous six months, but it was only a short visit to cut an album and promote the single 'Follow Me'.

It was nine years almost to the day since the release of her first Decca single and some 12 years since her first vocal ventures in public.

Below: In easy-listening Olivia's well-groomed image ensured success.

Roger Miller: Country Jester

In the late '50s and early '60s, certain artists were striving to inject a little more individuality and drive into the country music industry by cutting gutsy ballads with a distinct folk flavour like 'Four Strong Winds', 'The Ballad Of Ira Hayes', 'Big Bad John', 'Wolverton Mountain', 'Sleepy-Eyed John' and 'Alabam'. Those songs crossed over into the pop field but it wasn't enough — Nashville badly needed a new personality to give its product a major boost.

That personality emerged in the shape of Roger Miller, an ex-fireman and hotel bell hop, who'd already written one or two pleasant but unpretentious songs for artists like Ray Price, Ernest Tubb and Jim Reeves.

Miller, born in Texas but raised in Oklahoma, had been a keen student of music since his childhood and, following a frustrating period when he worked at a variety of mundane jobs, he decided to travel to Nashville and attempt to break into the music business. He was lucky because, coupled with a natural musical ability, Miller knew what he wanted and almost immediately found a job as a drummer with established stars like Faron Young, Minnie Pearl and George Jones. Miller, in fact, collaborated on several songs with George Jones, including 'That's The Way I Feel'.

Miller's early songs provided him with a comfortable living in Nashville but he wasn't happy with his work, he was conscious of the triteness of the majority of the contemporary country songs and he wanted to be more inventive and ambitious with his own lyrics.

In addition to writing songs like 'Invitation To The Blues', 'Poor Little John', 'Half A Mind' and 'Home' for artists like Ray Price, Ernest Tubb and Jim Reeves, Miller began to create more sophisticated material, but Nashville wasn't ready for it. Creative frustration eventually forced him to record his own material and in 1964 'Dang Me' and 'Chug-A-Lug' were released. Humour was Miller's particular forte, a sophisticated zaniness that added a new dimension to country music. The naive and often juvenile humour of the rural country comedians had made little impact on the American nation, but Miller's fusion of memorable tunes and his unique wit caused a sensation and in 1964 he received a total of five Grammy Awards for the million-selling infectious song 'Dang Me'.

The song was a 'talking blues' in the traditions of Robert Lunn, Woody Guthrie and Ramblin' Jack Elliott. The humour wasn't immediately apparent, although the structure of the song was interspersed with what might best be described as a form of 'scat' singing. The backing tracks were pure old-time country, with emphasis on the bass strings of the acoustic guitar, and Miller's voice was gritty.

The song that established Roger Miller on an international basis was 'King Of The Road', a story centred around the legendary American hoboes. In May 1965, the single reached no. 1 in the British hit parade and that same year Miller received a further six Grammy Awards for Best Contemporary Recording, Best Contemporary Vocal Performance (R&R — Male), Best C&W Recording (single), Best C&W Album, Best C&W Vocal Performance (Male) and Best C&W Song (Writers Award). Roger Miller had given Nashville and country music the boost it needed.

Drink And Depression

Miller's humour wasn't confined to his songs. On television chat shows and personal appearances he displayed a gift for sparkling wit and instant communication with his audience. Roger Miller had finally arrived.

The hits continued, many becoming classics, placing Miller in the same songwriting league as Hank Williams. The hits included 'Engine Engine Number 9', 'Kansas City Star', 'One Dyin' And A-Buryin'' and the delightful 'England Swings'. The latter song entered the British charts in 1966 and two years later Miller had his third British hit with the wistful 'Little Green Apples', a song composed by Bobby Russell.

Miller was equally at home singing deeply emotional ballads like 'One Dyin' And A-Buryin'' as he was with his humorous songs, the former style possibly reflecting his true personality. William Price Fox, who wrote the controversial country music novel *Ruby Red*, said of Miller: "It's as if his skin is too tight for him. He can spot insincerity from twenty yards. He is used to it. He is sad about it." Fox also wrote that Miller was like no other and that "depression rides him like a monkey."

Until 1971 Miller continued to make best-selling records, and following on from 'England Swings' came 'Husbands And Wives', 'Vance', 'Me And Bobby McGee', 'Where Have All The Average People Gone', 'Tom Green County Fair' and 'Tomorrow Night In Baltimore', but the initial genius had faded somewhat and by 1971 Miller was considered to be past his prime as a creative writer.

Rumours were rife for a time and there were hints of a period of personal problems and of increasing bouts of depression. By 1972 Miller was remembered only for his past hits and for a time he drifted into relative obscurity.

An album entitled 'Roger Miller 1970' and released that year had already shown that whatever he had had to say in the past had been said. Of the 11 titles, only one, 'I Know Who It Is', was credited to Miller, the remainder being composed by Bob Lind, Kris Kristofferson and others.

In 1973 the Miller talent resurfaced for the Walt Disney cartoon production, *Robin Hood*. Miller's voice and songs were used for the character of Allan-a-Dale but the movie wasn't one of Disney's best, and while several of Miller's contributions, including the brilliant 'Whistle Stop', were memorable, it failed to re-establish him as a star.

A previous movie, *Ballad Of Water Hole No. 3*, was also poorly received by the critics and although Miller's contributions to this particular production were confined only to the theme, it was an earlier indication of his falling status.

1973 also saw the release of an album wryly entitled 'Dear Folks Sorry I Haven't Written Lately'. Sadly, it served only to remind his many fans of how brilliant he had been in the past. There were hints of Miller's true genius contained in tracks like 'The Day I Jumped From Uncle Harvey's Plane' and 'Whistle Stop' but the remainder was dull and uninspired.

Miller, obviously very conscious of his absence from the music scene, flew to England in 1973 to appear in concert at a London theatre and to promote his speaking and singing-only role in *Robin Hood*. His concert was highly acclaimed and there were definite signs that the old fire had been re-kindled. Miller told various interviewers that his ideas had run dry and he'd nothing more to say for a while, hence the album 'Dear Folks'.

The year 1975 saw another re-emergence in the shape of an album called 'Supersongs' and one track 'Wanda Iguana', brought the Roger Miller of yesteryear back into prominence with 'scat' singing and zaniness, coupled with a funky, close-to-the-soil country sound. The rest of the album was still a departure from Miller's familiar territory, however and it seemed unlikely that he would ever emulate the success of those formative years with Smash Records.

Revolutionary Style

Miller earned a fortune from songwriting and as long as people remember tunes like 'You Had A Do-Wacka–Do', 'You Can't Roller Skate In A Buffalo Herd', 'Kansas City Star', 'My Uncle Used To Love Me But She Died' and 'Burma Shave', he will have a place in country music history.

Nashville and the whole of the country music industry reaped the benefits of Roger Miller's unique gift. His style of songwriting and singing was revolutionary and because so much talent flowed from him in the relatively brief space of four or five years, he could be forgiven for retreating into partial obscurity. In a sense Miller's songs were ahead of their time in terms of country music; the humour and lyrical intensity gave the genre far more

respectability than it had attained in years.

Unlike so many other country artists, Roger Miller realized the value of money the minute he tasted success with 'Invitation To The Blues' in 1958. It was one of the first of his songs to be picked up by another artist, in this case Ray Price. Miller was shrewd with his earnings and ultimately invested much of it in a hotel in Nashville, the King Of The Road. His philosophy was simple but wry: ''You have to diversify yourself and try to salt your money away for your old age. I never plan to be old but I do plan to be *rich*!''

Miller's formula for success clearly worked. Ringo Starr paid him the compliment of recording Miller's 'Husbands And Wives' on his 1975 'Goodbye Vienna' album, thus showing that Miller's talents were by no means overlooked in the mid-'70s rock music medley.

Left: Whooping it up — Roger Miller in the studio displaying the satirical humour that made his songs so well-known.

SKR

Chet Atkins

Chet Atkins once told a journalist: "There are a dozen young guitarists in this town (Nashville) who can do anything with a guitar that I can do. I don't try to stay ahead of them anymore. I just try to come up with an innovation occasionally, which I can apply to my kind of music. These new kids are good. I'm in a position now where I can help them."

Atkins is known primarily as a guitar virtuoso and is acknowledged as being one of the world's greatest exponents of the instrument, along with John Williams and Segovia. His instrumental accomplishments, however, take second place to his role as a record producer and part-creator of the Nashville Sound.

Born in Luttrell, East Tennessee, in 1924, Chet claims to have been influenced by the playing of Merle Travis and, later, George Barnes. Chet's father was a local piano teacher and his grandfather played the fiddle with some skill and the youngster chose to play the violin. It wasn't until he was about nine years old that Chet began to take a marked interest in the guitar and this he attributes to his half-brother Jim, yet another family instrumentalist. Jim had sung and played the guitar for many years and occasionally allowed Chet to pick out a few chords and melodies. Jim's encouragement, added to the seeds already sown by Merle Travis's radio sessions, persuaded Chet to take the instrument seriously.

Atkins initially modelled his style on the playing of Merle Travis but developed his own characteristic method. "You don't sit down and invent a new way to play the guitar," he once said.

The late Steve Sholes, who gave Atkins his first RCA recording contract during the 1940s described the musician's style thus: "Chet plays finger-style guitar. He doesn't pick; he just touches the strings, pushes down on them and lets his fingers up, except for his thumb — he has a pick on his thumb, and that's generally for the bass strings. He can play other styles too, Spanish, classical, everything else. But the style that first got me intrigued was his finger-style playing."

Chet's first job as a musician came in 1941 with radio station WNOX, in Knoxville, Tennessee, where he was employed as a fiddler and played with Archie Campbell and Bill Carlisle and the Dixieland Swingers. From WNOX he moved to WRGL, Columbus, Georgia, returned to the original Knoxville station in 1942 and then eventually joined KWTO in Springfield, Missouri, in 1949. During these years Atkins alternated between guitar and fiddle but, by the time he made

An acknowledged guitar virtuoso, Chet Atkins became a hit record producer.

his first recordings for the Bullet label, he was earning a reputation as a guitarist.

In 1947, Sholes signed Chet to RCA Victor and his first disc for the label was a vocal entitled 'Money, Marbles and Chalk', composed by Pop Eckler, but Atkins's days as a singer were short-lived.

RCA's catalogue now contains over 60 albums by Atkins and few of them fall strictly into the country music vein. Atkins doesn't like to be pigeon-holed and prefers to be described as a guitarist. Some of the titles he has recorded over the years show the diversity of his talents and they include 'Trambone', 'Chopin's Waltz No. 10', 'Zorba's Dance', 'Minute Waltz', 'Choro Da Saudade', 'Limehouse Blues', 'Liebestraum', 'How High The Moon', 'Love Theme From *The Godfather*' and 'Black Mountain Rag'.

Atkins has never considered himself to be a *country* guitarist and his early guest appearances at the Grand Ole Opry were not entirely successful as audiences in those early days (circa 1950) were reluctant to accept a solo guitarist.

Whereas Chet Atkins's musical contributions to country music were sporadic, his technical skill as a producer resulted in some of the most successful country singles and albums during the late '50s, the '60s and the '70s. Atkins had never been reluctant to provide guitar fills on various productions and his work can be heard on records by Skeeter Davis and Jimmie Driftwood.

Together with Owen Bradley and Ken Nelson, Atkins virtually salvaged what was left of country following the initial rock & roll onslaught of 1954. When rock finally emerged from the embryonic stages of rockabilly, country music talent in the United States was almost wiped out and those artists that couldn't adapt were left to flounder in a sea of uncertainty. Atkins and his two compatriots saw the obvious potential still left in Nashville as a recording centre of importance. As far back as the '20s the city had been used as a focal point for country recordings but it wasn't until Atkins, Owens and Nelson created their Nashville Sound that Nashville itself became an important musical centre and ultimately RCA invited Atkins to take charge of their Nashville operations. As a direct result of Atkins's affiliation with RCA and Nashville the city began to prosper.

Relaxed Southern Mood

Owen Bradley, who opened his Nashville studio in 1955 defined the Nashville Sound as: "Two German echo chambers turned wide open. We have a certain kind of player here, a certain kind of song. We also use a generous echo, which helps to cover mistakes." But according to Chet Atkins there is no such thing as the Nashville Sound, it's simply a result of the relaxed mood of the Southern musicians used on the sessions and the ultimate choice of material.

"The song's the thing," said Atkins. "You can have the biggest and most expensive studio, the best-sounding musicians, and expert engineers and technicians, but if you don't have the song, the artists can't be expected to have a hit."

The Nashville Sound has been successful because it incorporates the best of pop and country, using the same relaxed Southern pickers. Atkins's name has been attached to many country hits that have overspilled into the pop market. Of Skeeter Davis, one of RCA's earliest pop-country chart contenders: "She's a good example of how we've been able to bring pop to country. I always thought she had a chance for pop, so we took out the steel guitar and fiddles and made her a little more 'uptown' with her over-dubbing of the harmony, and she's done very well." Skeeter's most successful pop-country disc was, in fact, 'End Of The World' released in 1963.

Atkins was also directly responsible for taking the 'hillbilly' out of Jim Reeves's voice and replacing it with a laid-back (for those days) ballad style.

Pop-Country Channels

The basis of the Nashville Sound was a slip-note piano, attributed to Floyd Cramer and by 1960 it was estimated that Cramer's style was being featured on a quarter of all the American hit recordings, including those by Elvis Presley and Pat Boone. Other important elements that contributed to the overall acceptance of this new commercial country sound were vocal groups like the Anita Kerr Singers and the Jordanaires, who appeared on virtually every Nashville production, and the heavy rhythm guitar sounds forming the foundation to the songs.

Chet Atkins was always quick to comment on the 'sales potential' of his recordings and was aware of the need to keep ahead with new sounds and innovations. He realized that a vast 'countrypolitan' audience had to be catered for and that if country music were to go anywhere it would have to be through pop-country channels.

Capitol became the first major label to establish operations in Nashville, largely due to the awareness of Ken Nelson, but RCA, Decca and Columbia were quick to follow suit and, in spite of the claims of various musical pundits that Nelson, Owens, Don Law and one or two others were the first to organize the country market into a viable prospect, it was Chet Atkins who undoubtedly tied it all together.

Atkins was reputed to own half of Nashville and although this might be overstating the man's wealth, there can be little doubt that he was immensely wealthy. Only four of his vast output of albums for RCA have ever been deleted and his creative production work for the label continued unabated. Other RCA producers like Ronnie Light and Bob Ferguson had taken the attention off Atkins to some degree but Atkins was still the one the world remembers.

Emmylou Harris

''What I'm trying to do is play country music with a rock attitude. You just play it and you play it full volume and full force and you really kick ass 'cause country music is really ballsy music.''

Emmylou Harris once summed up her attitude to her music with these positive words. Perhaps the force with which she put her case was belied by her slight, winnowy, very feminine appearance. But such a seemingly fragile body can express all the elements of modern country — from the hard-driving of Merle Haggard's songs to the poignancy of Dolly Parton's 'Coat Of Many Colors'.

Country Merger

Emmylou Harris brought together the two faces of modern country as perhaps no other artist could. She managed to express the harder-edged work of rock-influenced performers while always returning to her favourites among more conventional country music. She managed to walk a very fine line between two different and often antagonistic forms, each with their own very vocal, very critical supporters. One of the tragedies of modern country has been bitter disputes between the more conservative old-time Nashvillers who decried the introduction of electric guitars, rock forms and modern lyrics and the 'country-rockers' who sneered at the traditionalists as 'dude cowboys' and 'nasal twangers'. In fact, each had more in common with the other than they realized and it took someone like Emmylou Harris with her charm, obvious talent and gentleness to show that there could be a middle ground.

She realized that the schizophrenia of modern country was reflected in her own attitudes. ''I prefer to keep my stuff pure,'' she once told an interviewer. "I'm a purist. I really am." But she added that: "I'm definitely not going to put out an album like Tammy Wynette" and that "I'll never tease my hair and put on a sequined dress, but I don't get uptight at people who do. It's just my personal taste." She also stated that she doesn't really believe in 'country-rock' as a fusion. "I love country music and I love rock music and I don't see why you have to put them together and get something less than what the two of them are separately."

Catholic Choice

Her music was formed by some very strong influences that seemed to conflict but which she was able to mesh together and weld into a very individualistic approach. She was most radically influenced by Gram Parsons — ex-Byrd, ex-Flying Burrito Brother, singer/song-writer (of genius, some vociferously claim) and tragic early victim of the rock lifestyle. At the same time she could assert that her favourite singer was George Jones — "the greatest country singer" — and nominate as preferred listening artists as diverse as Tanya Tucker and Steeleye Span, Stevie Wonder and Don Williams.

Perhaps a key to all these separate forces at work within her can be found in her early life which was almost that of a latterday gypsy. She was born in Birmingham, Alabama in 1949, the daughter of a Service family whose career took them all over the States. At high school her first ambition was to be an actress but she was seemingly rather an inhibited child — she later claimed that she was the one girl who never got asked out on dates, which anyone who has seen her fine-boned features will find hard to believe — and was too embarrassed to act. She had been singing for a while but didn't consider that she had any special aptitude for it — "I thought I had a pleasant voice but I never really thought of myself as a singer."

While other young people at the time were toting their guitars round campus coffee shops, playing folk for pennies in a basket, Emmylou was poring over her books and showing the sort of academic promise that distinguished one of her fellow country artists — Kris Kristofferson. She applied herself so assiduously to her studies that she won a clutch of prizes for history, English and essay writing. ("No wonder I never got any dates!") Eventually, however, the lure of the folksinger's life proved too strong and she found herself in New York at the end of the Greenwich village folk boom. Like so many others of her generation she was taken by the Woody Guthrie-inspired dream of the modern wandering minstrel: "I was very enamoured by the whole idea of travelling around with my guitar . . . and discovering all these things that I'd missed."

Although she was too late to benefit from the upsurge in folk music, she fell in with some of the many young musicians who were flooding into New York at the time. Through friends like Jerry Jeff Walker (composer of 'Mr. Bojangles') and others she was drawn more than ever towards music, introduced to country and, eventually, was signed to make an album for the Jubilee label. It was entitled 'Gliding Bird' and described by Emmylou, in retrospect, as "a disaster." It contained five of her own songs but instead of being as she hoped — "pure and wonderful and beautiful" — it turned out very unrepresentative of her work. This was probably due to the fact that she was entirely inexperienced in the record business and allowed others to take control.

Broken Marriage

All the while she was getting more and more interested in country and even made a trip to Nashville where her attempts to fuse the new and traditional were not yet accepted by the diehards. This was evidently a difficult stage in her life because around that time she married. The union lasted only for a year and broke up leaving her with a daughter, Hallie, to support.

After a time she gravitated towards Washington where she started playing the circuit of bars and gaining a great deal of essential experience; more important, after her recent confusions, she was "able to re-discover why I got into music in the first place" and work out some of the conflicting styles within her.

The most significant musical meeting of her life occurred in Washington. She had got to know the Flying Burritos and was invited to join them shortly before they broke up. Despite this disappointment, the

Below: Gram Parsons, the musical mentor who transformed Emmylou's life and whose tragic death filled her with zeal.

band introduced her to one of their ex-members, Gram Parsons.

Some time after meeting and playing a couple of gigs with Emmylou Harris in Washington, he contacted her and asked if she'd sing on his first solo album — 'GP'. This was the start of an intense musical relationship that packed two albums (the other was the posthumously released 'Grievous Angel'), a tour and the altering of Emmylou Harris's life into a very short time.

Her time working with Parsons was so important that his influence was to pervade everything she did, musically, for years after his death. ''Gram Parsons was a real pioneer,'' she once told an interviewer. ''He cut straight through the middle with no compromise. He wrote some of the most beautiful songs I've ever heard.'' She went out of her way to acknowledge the debt she owed him and to fulfill a self-imposed mission — ''If there's one thing in my life I really have to do, it's to get Gram's music out in the open where it should be.''

Parsons's untimely death on September 19, 1973 — the cause was, officially, ''over-stimulation of the heart'' and his body was reportedly cremated in the desert in accordance with his wishes — shattered Emmylou. She started working with a desperation. She went back to Washington, formed a group, wrote songs and used the activity as therapy. She had made an impact on the two Parsons records, however, and landed a contract with Reprise records which resulted in her first solo album, 'Pieces Of The Sky'.

Intriguing Mix

'Pieces Of The Sky' represented a mix of music and style — with a predominantly country feel — that was intriguing. It included Merle Haggard's booze-soaked, regretful 'The Bottle Let Me Down' (''the kind of song I used to do all the time when working in the bars''), 'Sleepless Nights', an old Everly Brothers' song, Dolly Parton's auto-biographical 'Coat Of Many Colours' (''my favourite song'' and dedicated on the album to Parsons's sister), Lennon and McCartney's 'For No One' and, a roistering version of 'Queen Of The Silver Dollar' among others.

Perhaps surprisingly, the album only contained one of Emmylou's own songs — 'Boulder To Birmingham'. But it is a significant song expressing, as it does, so many of the emotions that assailed her after Parsons's death and as a result of seeing a serious fire in Topango Canyon. ''It's a strange, strange song,'' she once admitted. ''I felt perfectly miserable and alone but somehow the song came together out of all these things.'' It was written with Bill Danoff — ''he helped me with the melody on the verses'' — a close friend and associate of John Denver with whom he wrote 'Take Me Home, Country Roads'.

Although Emmylou was virtually unknown to the general record-buying public, a word of mouth campaign caused a great deal of interest in the album and quite quickly it was being bought in enormous quantities. This surprised its creator as much as anyone. ''I figured it would be ignored,'' she said, ''cause it wasn't a commercial pop record and it wasn't a basic country album. And it definitely wasn't a rock & roll album.''

Interest in this new young singer who seemed to marry rock and country with such aplomb grew fast and more records and appearances were demanded. Her follow-up album was even more successful both commercially and musically. It was called 'Elite Hotel' and repeated the successful mix of new and old. Gram Parsons's influence was evident with the inclusion of three of his songs; the traditional side was well supported with numbers from Buck Owens, Don Gibson and Hank Williams; and Lennon and McCartney were represented by a superb version of 'Here, There And Everywhere'.

The album was particularly strong in its contributors with instrumental support from such luminaries as James Burton, Glen D. Hardin, Bill Payne from Little Feat, Bernie Leadon of the Eagles, ex-Dillard Herb Pederson and vocal help from Linda Ronstadt. When she came to tour, Emmylou was able to reflect this wealth of talent in her group — the Hot Band. The line-up included both Burton — who had played with Rick Nelson and had been, with Hardin, a regular member of Elvis Presley's touring group — who was fast becoming a 'guitar hero' and Hardin. The latter had played with Buddy Holly before he was a star and became a member of the Crickets after Holly's death. In addition there was Rodney Crowell — who co-wrote 'Amarillo' with Emmylou and also contributed 'Till I Gain Control Again' to her second album — and the amazingly talented pedal-steel player Hank diVito. The partnership of Emmylou and the Hot Band on concert dates was inspired and added greatly to her fast-burgeoning success. Together they made what Glen Hardin described as ''a nice clean modern kind of country.''

Emmylou Harris managed to pull together, to act as a bridge between, the twin, but disparate, strands of country. She stood between diehard Nashville on the one hand and the more radical but still country-based work of men like Kris Kristofferson and John Prine on the other. Her bitter-sweet approach — ''sad songs are more fun to sing'' — appealed to both the rock audience that was just being introduced to country and the more traditional elements who held Tammy Wynette as their queen. This wasn't to say that she fell between the two, Emmylou Harris was nothing if not her own woman and she offered a style and an artistry that were uniquely individual.

The Grand Ole Opry

America's longest-running country music radio programme, the *Grand Ole Opry*, is a cultural institution and a vigorous part of the nation's colourful history. The *Grand Ole Opry* was conceived by George Dewey Hay, a one-time news reporter for the *Memphis Commercial Appeal*. One of Hay's assignments as a newspaper-man involved the tracking down of a First World War veteran who lived in the foothills of the Ozark Mountains, near Mammoth Springs, Arkansas. After locating and interviewing his quarry and subsequently filing his story, Hay was invited to attend a hoe-down in a cabin "lighted by a coal-oil lamp."

Hay, who had apparently always been sympathetic towards folk music, described the hoedown in this manner: "It carried on until the crack o' dawn and no one has ever had more fun than those Ozark mountaineers had that night. It stuck with me until the idea became the *Grand Ole Opry* seven or eight years later."

In 1923 the Solemn Old Judge (as Hay was known) resigned as a reporter and became radio editor with the Commercial Appeal Radio Station. He was good enough at his job to be asked the following year to produce a Barn Dance programme on station WLS, in Chicago. He accepted the position and within a few months had organized the *WLS Barn Dance*, later to become famous throughout the States as the *National Barn Dance*.

George Hay left WLS on October 5th, 1925 and took up office as director of WSM Radio, in Nashville, Tennessee. Memories of the old hoedown in the Ozarks still haunted him persistently and within six months of joining WSM, Hay had launched the station's first *Barn Dance* programme.

National Boom

At 8.00 pm on Saturday, November 28th, 1925, George Hay introduced the *WSM Barn Dance* to the tune of the tradtional 'Tennessee Waggoner', performed by Uncle Jimmy Thompson, an 82-year-old Civil War veteran, who claimed to know a thousand tunes and could "fiddle the bugs off a sweet tater vine." Thompson had been introduced to Hay the previous evening by Eva Thompson Jones, the fiddle player's daughter. Eva was an accomplished pianist and she accompanied her father on that historic broadcast.

Contrary to popular belief, Uncle Jimmy Thompson was not the sole performer on George Hay's first *WSM Barn Dance*. In addition to Eva Thompson Jones, the performers also included Burt Hutcherson, Staley Walton and Alcyon Bate. Uncle Jimmy, however, earned 'star billing' due to his advanced age and actually played continuously for over an hour, stopping only when persuaded to make way for the other performers.

Much to George Hay's surprise Uncle Jimmy Thompson proved an immediate success and after the inaugural programme WSM's studios were literally besieged by performers eager to get in on the act. Thompson's photograph was carried on the front page of the *Nashville Tennessean* newspaper and fiddle playing suddenly developed into a national boom.

From the hundreds of performers who applied to WSM for auditions, Hay selected 25, including Mrs. Cline, a talented and enthusiastic zither player, the Crook Brothers (Lewis and Herman), the Fruit Jar Drinkers, the Gully Jumpers and Dr Humphrey Bate, a graduate of Vanderbilt University, who performed on the harmonica and was later to form a highly respected string band, the Possum Hunters. Dr Bate, a Tennessee physician, had served with the Army during the

Spanish-American War and led a mountain band as early as 1900. Bate's Possum Hunters became the first real 'hillbilly' band to appear on what was soon to become the *Grand Ole Opry*.

For the first year of its distinguished life the *WSM Barn Dance* was ostensibly a showcase for instrumentalists, although several of the ballads featured by these musicians from time to time called for a vocal refrain of sorts. In 1926, however, George Hay engaged the services of the programme's first singing star, Uncle Dave Macon an adroit banjo player and vocalist from the Cannon County hills of Tennessee. Macon was 56 years old when he joined the cast of the Barn Dance, following a successful career in vaudeville; he brought with him a wide variety of complex banjo playing styles and a seemingly endless repertoire of mountain ballads and folk songs.

"All my life I played and sung for fun," he once told an interviewer, "and my neighbours always asked me to play at picnics and special occasions. Finally, one self-important farmer approached me and asked me to play at a party he was planning. I was very busy and a bit tired, so I thought I would stop him. I told him I'd play at his party for $15. He said, 'Okay, it's a deal.' It was a large affair and in the crowd was a talent scout for Loew's Theatres. My act seemed to go over very well. When I had finished, the theatre man offered to book me at a leading theatre in Birmingham, Alabama, at several hundred dollars a week. They held me over many weeks and booked me throughout the country. I was in the show-business and I have been ever since." Once described as the "King of the Hillbillies" but affectionately known as "The Dixie Dewdrop", Uncle Dave Macon remained a top attraction on the *Grand Ole Opry* for 15 years and not until 1938, when Roy Acuff and his Smokey Mountain Boys joined the show did he take a subordinate position in the cast.

Earthy Rebellion

On December 10, 1927, the *WSM Barn Dance* became officially known as the *Grand Ole Opry* and by this time the programme had increased to a three-hour event, which followed a NBC production, *The Musical Appreciation Hour,* conducted by Dr Walter Damrosch.

At the end of one such programme Damrosch concluded with these words: "While most artists realize that there is no place in the classics for realism, I am going to break one of my rules and present a composition by a young composer from Iowa. This young man has sent us his latest composition, which depicts the onrush of a locomotive. . . ."

George Hay listened to Damrosch's words and when he introduced the *Barn Dance* that same evening, he retorted: "Dr Damrosch told us it was generally agreed that there is no place in the classics for realism. However, from here on out for the next three hours we will present

nothing but realism. It will be down to earth for the earthy. In respectful contrast to Dr Damrosch's presentation of the number which depicts the onrush of a locomotive, we will call on one of our performers, DeFord Bailey, with his harmonica to give us the country version of his 'Pan American'."

At the end of Bailey's piece, Hay resumed by adding: "For the past hour we have been listening to music taken largely from Grand Opera . . . but from now on we will present the 'Grand Ole Opry'."

Golden Roster

DeFord Bailey, a one-time lift operator and the first Negro to appear on the *Grand Ole Opry*, featured 'Pan American' as the show's signature tune for the next 15 years. Although Bailey remained on the programme for such a long period, he was apparently reluctant to learn more than a handful of tunes and Hay was obliged to dispense with his services. The Negro's 'limited repertoire', if such was the case, consisted of standard and 'traditional' hillbilly tunes, which included 'The Fox Chase', 'Alcoholic Blues', 'The Old Hen Cackled', 'Ice Water Blues' and 'Davidson County Blues'.

After his dismissal from the *Opry*, DeFord Bailey drifted into obscurity and was last heard of in 1965 operating a shoeshine stand in Nashville. During his time with WSM he did, however, become one of the very first artists to record in Nashville. On September 28, 1928, he cut several sides for RCA Victor and later recorded various tracks for Vocalion, Brunswick and Columbia.

In an attempt to accommodate a larger studio audience the *Grand Ole Opry* moved from WSM's Studio 'A', to the Hillsboro Theater but almost immediately the seating capacity was found to be totally inadequate. A move to a tabernacle on the seedy east bank of the Cumberland river came next but due to its unsavoury location, the building was abandoned and the Tennessee War Memorial Auditorium was rented.

The *Grand Ole Opry* had become an overwhelming success and as a measure of audience control an admission fee of 25 cents was introduced in 1939. Weekly attendances were averaging 3000 and the *Grand Ole Opry* had been on the air for 14 uninterrupted years. Hay summed up the popularity of the *Opry* and country music in general when he said: "It is as fundamental as sunshine and rain, snow and wind and the light of the moon peeping through the trees. Some folks like it and some dislike it very much, but it'll be there long after you and I have passed out of this picture for the next one. . . ."

Acts now included Curly Fox, a fiddler of national prominence, whose instrumental recording 'Black Mountain Rag' had sold over 600,000 copies, Texas Ruby (who later perished in a fire), Jimmy Brown, Asher Sizemore & Little Jimmy, Fiddlin' Arthur Smith and His Dixieliners,

C.I.C.

Opposite: crowds queue up for an afternoon performance of the *Grand Ole Opry*, and (insert) Roy Acuff in a 1948 show. Right: Hank Snow (above) and Bobby Bare, two of the *Opry*'s great stars from a show that spawned hundreds of hits.

Ernest Tubb and his Texas Troubadours, one of the many famous _Grand Ole Opry_ acts.

the Binkley Brothers (who were the very first artists to record in Nashville in 1928), Uncle Ed Poplin and His Old Timers, Zeke Clements, Bill Monroe and His Bluegrass Boys, Ernest Tubb and his Texas Troubadours, Claude Lampley, the Cackle Sisters, Smilin' Jack and His Missouri Mountaineers, the Delmore Brothers, Sam & Kirk McGee, Roy Acuff and the Smokey Mountain Boys, Jamup and Honey, Theron Hale, Nap and Dee, Pap Wilson, Dozie Ramer and Pee Wee King and His Golden West Cowboys.

The two most notable performers of this period in _Grand Ole Opry_ and country music development were undoubtedly Roy Acuff and accordionist-bandleader Pee Wee King. They were wholly responsible for the transition from a band featuring a singer, to a vocalist accompanied by a band. The former had been the accepted practice since the _Opry's_ inception in 1925. Singers like Uncle Dave Macon had been featured on the show but not in the same context.

Acuff, a former baseball player, and his band the Smokey Mountain Boys, joined the _Opry_ in 1938 but they made little impression until 1940, when they performed a gospel song, 'The Great

Speckled Bird'. Prior to this the band had performed as a single unit, with little or no emphasis being placed on any one member. Following a relatively uneventful two years on the show Acuff decided to reorganize the structure of his group and place more prominence on himself as a vocalist. With songs like 'The Great Speckled Bird', 'Radio Station S-A-V-E-D' and 'Wabash Cannonball', Acuff and his band became country music sensations and within the space of three years he was earning the staggering sum of $200,000 a year!

Roy Acuff became the first to give country singers a status above that of the band but Pee Wee King completed the transition. Featured in King's western-flavoured band was Eddy Arnold, a guitarist who often 'doubled' as a vocalist. One evening in 1939, Arnold was called upon to perform a number entitled 'Mommy, Please Stay Home With Me'. The resulting applause was deafening and Arnold had arrived as a country music vocalist in no uncertain terms. From that point on country music was to undergo vast changes. Gone were the crowds of banjo pickers and fiddlers hoping to be 'discovered'; they were replaced by a

deluge of vocalists, each one hoping to emulate Arnold's sudden success. With the popularity of 'Mommy, Please Stay Home With Me', Eddy Arnold left the Golden West Cowboys, adopted the title, The Tennessee Plowboy, and formed a band.

The ever-increasing popularity of country music led one again to seating capacity problems at the _Grand Ole Opry_ but in 1941, a permanent home was found at the Ryman Auditorium, which later became known as Opry House and housed the world-famous country music show until the beginning of the 1970's, when it moved, for the last time, to a new multi-million dollar complex known as Opryland.

New Opryland

By the mid-'60s, it had become apparent to all concerned that the elderly Ryman building was outmoded and totally unsuited to the requirements of modern country music. Few structural changes had been made to the building since 1892 (when it was built) and it was cold, damp and confined backstage. The final humiliation came when the old edifice was condemned as a fire-risk by Nashville's Fire Department. The giant Opryland complex gradually became a reality and the _Opry's_ once-illustrious home, the Ryman Auditorium, with its ghosts of a thousand country singers and pickers still echoing across the weathered stage, was suddenly doomed to become the victim of the wreckers' hammers.

The final move to Opryland was completed during the first years of the '70s and, whilst the old-timers like Sam McGee and Claude Lampley weren't too sure if it was the right move to make, the newer country stars quickly adapted to the new home. The _Grand Ole Opry_ has become an important part of America's musical culture and although the various changes of venue over the years have caused consternation among the traditionalists and preservationists, it's the spirit of the music reflected by the name that is important. Most of America's great country music stars have graced the _Opry's_ varied stages at one time or another – and they do it for prestige value rather than hard cash. The fees paid to _Opry_ performers barely cover expenses and the most an artist of Johnny Cash's calibre could expect to earn from a Saturday night appearance would be in the region of $60.

The _Opry_ has been called the Carnegie Hall of country music and its roll of honour includes such fabulous names as Tex Ritter, Hank Snow, Bobby Bare, Marty Robbins, Flatt & Scruggs, Don Reno, Kitty Wells, Loretta Lynn, Porter Wagoner and Dolly Parton, Stringbean, Bob Wills and His Texas Playboys, the Pickard Family, Hank Williams, George Jones, Patsy Cline, Grandpa Jones, Jim Reeves and others too numerous to mention.

George Dewey Hay, the man who first conceived the _Grand Ole Opry_ at a mountain hoedown so many years ago, may be dead and gone. But his creation remains the best country music show of them all.

Country Round-Up

ROY ACUFF: Born in Maynardsville, Tennessee, in 1903, Acuff began his long and distinguished career as the leader of a hillbilly band called Roy Acuff and His Crazy Tennesseans, working on radio stations WNOX and WROL in Knoxville, Tennessee. In 1936, Acuff made his first recordings for the Columbia label and the two titles from that initial session, 'The Great Speckled Bird' and 'Wabash Cannonball', later became country music classics.

In 1938 Acuff and his band joined the Grand Ole Opry and, following a rather unrewarding start, he changed the band's name to the Smokey Mountain Boys, employing Bashful Brother Oswald (Pete Kirby) on banjo, dobro and vocal harmonies. That year Oswald cut his first recordings with the Acuff band and gradually a unique and distinctive sound began to emerge, giving Acuff his first definite musical direction. He discarded most of the semi-pop novelties from his group's repertoire and began to feature traditional ballads in his act.

Acuff was best known for the aforementioned songs, together with 'The Old Age Pension Check', 'The Precious Jewel', 'Don't Make Me Go To Bed And I'll Be Good', 'Fireball Mail', 'Night Train To Memphis' and 'Wreck On The Highway'. In addition to his recording and performing activities, Acuff was also a partner in the mammoth Acuff-Rose publishing house, having formed the liaison with Fred Rose in 1942. In 1962 Acuff was elected to the Country Music Hall Of Fame. He recorded for the Hickory label, which he also owned.

REX ALLEN: Known as 'The Arizona Cowboy', Allen was born in Willcox, Arizona, in 1924, and after taking an electronics course at the University College of Los Angeles, worked on a cattle ranch as a cowhand. Allen was best known for 'Take It Back And Change It For A Boy', 'Money, Marbles And Chalk', 'Crying In The Chapel' and 'Don't Go Near The Indians'. During 1949, his CBS radio show was at no. 7 in the US ratings. His voice was heard on numerous documentaries produced by Walt Disney.

BILL ANDERSON: Born in Columbia, South Carolina, in 1937, Anderson was one of the most prolific songwriters of the '60s and '70s and an American trade journal named him as one of the three all-time greatest country music songwriters. A former sports writer for a newspaper, Anderson recorded for MCA and became internationally famous for compositions like 'City Lights',

'Riverboat', 'The Tips Of My Fingers', 'Po' Folks', 'Still', '8 X 10', 'Saginaw Michigan' and 'Cincinnati, Ohio'. On February 12, 1975, Anderson participated in broadcasting history when the concert he appeared in at the Hippodrome, Golders Green, London, was recorded by the BBC and transmitted to the United States via satellite.

EDDY ARNOLD: Became one of the most influential country vocalists during the '40s. Arnold was a member of Pee Wee King's Golden West Cowboys when, in 1939, he became the first singer to emerge from a subordinate position with a band to be accepted as a vocalist in his own right. Known originally as 'The Tennessee Plowboy', Arnold was born in 1918 near

Henderson, Tennessee. During his heyday Arnold virtually re-shaped the course of country (and western) music and he is reputed to have sold in excess of 60 million records during his career, among the most popular being 'Bouquet Of Roses', 'Texerkana Baby', 'Anytime', 'I Really Don't Want To Know', 'Cattle Call' and 'Tennessee Stud'.

ASLEEP AT THE WHEEL: A latter day western swing outfit partly responsible for the revival of interest in the music of the late Bob Wills. The band's most notable record was an album,

'Comin' Right At Ya', released on United Artists. The group's personnel comprised: Chris O'Connell, Ray Benson, Gene Dobkin, Floyd Domino, Reuben Gosfield and Leroy Preston.

BOBBY BARE: A native of Ohio, Bare's first musical success was 'All American Boy' which he recorded for the Fraternity label under the name of Bill Parsons in 1958. Following a two-year stint with the army, Bare joined RCA Victor and recorded a number of hits in the folk-country vein, including '500 Miles', 'Four Strong Winds' and 'Detroit City'. Bare left RCA for a period and signed with Mercury Records but later returned to RCA where he cut two classic albums, 'Lullabys, Legends And Lies' and 'Singin' In The Kitchen'. He also made an impressive acting debut in the western *A Distant Trumpet*.

BLUE SKY BOYS: Bill and Earl Bolick from Ashville, North Carolina, were a close harmony duo whose singing greatly influenced the structure of Bluegrass at the turn of the '40s. The repertoire of the Blue Sky Boys was largely derived from early folk ballads and included such traditional pieces as 'The Butcher Boy', 'Mary Of The Wild Moor' and 'Katie Dear'. After many successful years with the Bluebird and RCA Victor labels, Bill and Earl eventually parted company, but in 1963 were persuaded to return to the recording studios and cut some further titles for the now-defunct Starday label.

ELTON BRITT: Born 1920 in Marshall, Arkansas, he died in 1972. Britt, the son of a champion fiddler, was one of the world's greatest yodellers and his biggest contributions to country music were 'There's A Star Spangled Banner Waving Somewhere' and 'Chimebells'.

HYLO BROWN: Born in Paintsville, Kentucky, Brown began his professional career at the age of 16. He became bass player and featured vocalist with Lester Flatt and Earl Scruggs and the Foggy Mountain Boys. Brown then moved on to become a star of *The Original Jamboree*, broadcast from WWVA in Wheeling, West Virginia. Noted for his wide vocal range – hence the name Hylo – Brown was also associated with the near-legendary Lonesome Pine Fiddlers and fronted his own successful Bluegrass band, the Timberliners. Brown's most successful song was probably 'The Prisoner's Song'.

JIM ED BROWN: Brown was once tipped to succeed the late Jim Reeves but didn't quite make it. Although very successful as

a solo artist, he is possibly best remembered for his recordings with the Browns (a trio comprising Jim Ed, Maxine and Bonnie Brown) which included 'The Trot', 'I Heard The Bluebirds Sing', 'The Three Bells' (a world-wide hit in 1959) and 'Scarlet Ribbons'.

JIMMY BUFFETT: One of the new-breed of country song-writers Buffett hailed from Florida and wrote and recorded 'for

pleasure'. His most widely-known composition is 'Railroad Lady' recorded by Lefty Frizzell.

BILL CARLISLE: Born 1908 in Wakefield, Kentucky, Carlisle began recording on *The Carlisle Family Barn Dance* on Radio

WLAP in Louisville. For a number of years he performed with his brother Cliff as the Carlisle Brothers. Bill held over 60 different country music awards and among his most successful records were 'No Help Wanted', 'What Kinda Deal Is This' and 'Too Old To Cut The Mustard'.

JENKS 'TEX' CARMAN: One-time member of the famous Town Hall Party country show, Carman was a gifted but under-rated steel guitarist who achieved moderate success with 'Hillbilly Hula' and 'Locust Hill Rag'. Carman was born in 1911 and recorded for such labels as Capitol and 4-Star before his death.

CARTER FAMILY: The original Carter Family, one of country music's most influential early groups, consisted of Alvin Pleasant Carter, Sara Doherty Carter and Mother Maybelle Addison Carter. The group's many recordings, dating from July, 1927,

are highly revered. The Carters brought 'home music' to the masses and even the Depression had little effect on the sales of their countless records. A. P. Carter (1891–1960) was a prolific composer, though the main body of songs bearing his name appeared to be re-workings of traditional ballads.

Among the Carters' legendary records are 'Wildwood Flower', 'My Old Cottage Home', 'Amber Tresses', 'Green Fields Of Virginia' and 'My Clinch Mountain Home'. Sara Carter rarely made appearances after the '60s but Mother Maybelle was still very active and often worked with Johnny Cash. Her daughter June Carter was married to Cash and his roadshow usually featured a Carter Family cameo performed by June, Mother Maybelle and Anita Carter.

ROY CLARK: Comedian, multi-instrumentalist and master showman, Clark's contribution to country was considerable and his hits included 'Tips Of My Fingers', 'Yesterday When I Was Young'

and 'Thank God And Greyhound'. In 1973 the Country Music Association presented him with its Entertainer Of The Year award. He was born in Merherrin, Virginia.

SANFORD CLARK: One of the great mystery figures of rockabilly and country music he made the grade at the end of the '50s with 'The Fool', followed by 'Son Of A Gun', 'Run Boy Run' and 'Go On Home'. His early singles became eagerly sought-after by collectors.

PATSY CLINE: The late Patsy Cline's major breakthrough came when she performed 'Walkin' After Midnight' on the *Arthur Godfrey Show* in 1957. From that time until her death in a plane crash in 1963, Virginia-born Patsy earned international acclaim for hits like 'Crazy', 'I Fall To Pieces' and 'Sweet Dreams'. By the mid-'70s her records continued to sell steadily.

TOMMY COLLINS: From Oklahoma City, Collins achieved lasting fame as the result of his novelty hits 'It Tickles', 'You Better Not Do That', 'Whatcha Gonna Do Now' and 'You Gotta Have A Licence'. After his initial success Collins left the music business to become a preacher but later became musically active again. His best-known contemporary composition is 'The Man Who Picked The Wildwood Flower', recorded by Merle Haggard.

LLOYD 'COWBOY' COPAS: Born 1913 in Muskogee, Oklahoma. A former ranch and farm hand, Copas climbed to fame during the years immediately following World War II and became a member of the Grand Ole Opry in 1945. An outstanding and much-imitated flat-top guitarist, Cope (as he was known) was responsible for nine big country hits, including 'Tragic Romance', 'Filipino Baby', 'Signed, Sealed And Delivered' and 'Alabam'. Copas died in the same plane wreck that claimed the lives of Patsy Cline and Hawkshaw Hawkins in 1963.

BILLY 'CRASH' CRADDOCK: Notable for two big country hits, 'Knock Three Times' and 'Rub It In', Craddock, a North Carolinan, also achieved a fair measure of success as a rock & roll

artist before turning to country.

DICK CURLESS: For some reason Curless never quite made it to the top, though his hits were numerous. Main contributions: 'A Tombstone Every Mile', ''Tater Raisin' Man', 'Big Wheel

Cannonball', 'Drag 'Em Off The Interstate, Sock It To 'Em J. P. Blues'. In 1966 Curless became a member of Buck Owens's travelling show.

VERNON DALHART: Born Dalhart, Texas, in 1883, he began his career as an opera singer with the New York Light Opera Company but turned to hillbilly in 1924. Dalhart, whose real name was Marion T. Slaughter, teamed up with guitarist/songwriter Carson J. Robison and became enormously popular via such songs as 'Wreck Of The Southern Old 97', 'The Prisoner's Song' and 'The Runaway Train'. Dalhart drifted into almost total obscurity after the Depression and died in a cheap hotel in Bridgeport, Connecticut, where he was working as a night porter.

SKEETER DAVIS: Skeeter — real name Mary Francis Penick — was a former member of a duo known as the Davis Sisters. When her friend and partner, Betty Jack Davis, was killed in a road accident in 1953, Skeeter retired for several months but returned to recording and was very successful. Outside the country field

she was best known for 'End Of The World' which entered the British charts in 1963. Skeeter's other hits include 'Gonna Get Along Without You Now', 'One Tin Soldier' and 'Bus Fare To Kentucky'.

JIMMY DEAN: Born in Planview, Texas, in 1928, Dean's first hit record was 'Bummin' Around' on the 4-Star label in 1953. He later moved to Columbia Records and became one of the select band of country artists to attain overseas chart status on more than one occasion. Dean's first international hit was 'Big Bad John' and others included 'Little Black Book' and 'Cajun Queen'.

DELMORE BROTHERS: Alton and Rabon Delmore contributed greatly to the structure of country music with their folk and blues recordings. Alton, born in Elkmont, Alabama, in 1908, was a gifted songwriter and penned 'Brown's Ferry Blues', 'Gonna Lay Down My Old Guitar' and 'Blues Stay Away From Me'. He died in 1964. Rabon, also a songwriter, died in 1952 aged 36.

AL DEXTER: Born Jacksonville, Texas, in 1902, he became widely popular as a result of 'Pistol Packin' Mama', released on the Okeh label in 1943.

THE DILLARDS: Doug Dillard, Rodney Dillard, Mitch Jayne and Dean Webb. During the '60s the Ozark-based bluegrass band achieved wide critical acclaim.

After the group disbanded for a period, Doug Dillard merged talents with Gene Clark to form Dillard and Clark, backed by Chris Hillman, Sneaky Pete Kleinow and Bernie Leadon. The success of this musical aggregation was short-lived and Doug Dillard virtually vanished from the scene. The Dillards, in a semi-rock form, were later revived by Rodney who, together with Dean Webb, Mitch Jayne and Paul York among others, produced one or two interesting albums between 1968 and 1972. However, the best 'original' Dillards album was 'Backporch Bluegrass' issued in 1966.

JIMMIE DRIFTWOOD: Born Mountain View, Arkansas, 1918 and called 'America's Favourite Bard'. Reared in the Ozark Mountains of Arkansas, Driftwood (James Morris) absorbed the music and traditions of the early settlers in that area. In 1958 he signed with RCA and later wrote lyrics to 'Eighth Of January', an old fiddle tune, and re-titled it 'The Battle Of New Orleans'. He was also responsible for 'Sal's Got A Sugar Lip', 'Tennessee Stud', 'Soldier's Joy' and 'Unfortunate Man'. After 1966 Driftwood ceased recording and devoted much of his time to the Rackensack Folklore Society which he founded in 1963. Driftwood's albums can be found on RCA and Monument. His early classic, 'The Battle Of New Orleans', was revived in 1975 by the Nitty Gritty Dirt Band and Buck Owens.

THE EAGLES: The Byrds' 'Sweetheart Of The Rodeo' album recorded in 1968 inspired many other bands to experiment with electric country music, including Poco, the New Riders Of The Purple Sage and the most influential of them all, the Eagles. The Eagles comprised Randy Meisner (vocals, bass and guitar), Bernie Leadon (vocals, guitar, banjo, mandolin and dobro), Glenn Frey

(vocals, guitar, piano and harmonica) and Don Henley (vocals, drums and percussion). While they featured elements of country, particularly Bluegrass, in their recordings, the group had few real connections with country music. Their best-known tracks include 'Witchy Woman', 'Desperado', 'Take It Easy' and 'Lyin' Eyes'.

EVERLY BROTHERS: Had a phenomenal amount of hits, most of them heavily country-orientated. Don and Phil were born in Brownie, Kentucky, in 1937, and during their most productive years did more to popularize country music on a world-wide scale than any other act. Hits include: 'Bird Dog', 'Wake Up Little Susie', 'All I Have To Do Is Dream' and 'Bye Bye Love'.

FREDDY FENDER: The pseudonym of Baldemar G. Huerta who, until his success in country music, ran the whole gamut of popular music styles. Fender began his career playing Chicano music in and around the beer joints of San Benito, the Texas-Mexico border town where he was born. From Chicano he gradually changed to Tex-Mex rockabilly music and in 1959 recorded 'Wasted Days And Wasted Nights', his first hit. A second successful single, 'Crazy, Crazy Baby', followed and Fender's future seemed assured. On May 13, 1960, however, he was convicted on a drugs charge and sent to Angola State Prison for three years.

Upon his release he returned to the music scene and eventually met Cajun record producer Huey Meaux. In 1974 Freddy cut his first country disc, 'Before The Next Teardrop Falls', for Meaux's Crazy Cajun label and it became a huge national cross-over hit, finally establishing Fender as a major artist. He also re-recorded 'Wasted Days And Wasted Nights' and took it high into the country charts. Like fellow Mex-Tex artist Johnny Rodriguez, Fender sang many of his lyrics in Spanish.

LESTER FLATT: One-time guitarist and vocalist with Bill Monroe's Blue Grass Boys, Lester left the band, together with banjo player Earl Scruggs, and later formed their own group, the Foggy Mountain Boys. Lester and Earl's band eventually became the most commercially successful Bluegrass outfit in the history of country music and from 1959 until their split in 1969, recorded such best-sellers as 'The Ballad Of Jed Clampett', 'Petticoat Junction', 'Cabin On The Hill', 'California Uptight Band' and 'Foggy Mountain Breakdown'. In 1969, Lester began working with a new 'grass band called Nashville Grass. In 1975 he underwent extensive open heart surgery and at one period was close to death, but he recovered.

CLYDE JULIAN 'RED' FOLEY: Foley, who died in 1968 at the age of 58, was a former member of the Cumberland Ridge-runners, one of the first outfits to feature a squaredance group. In later years Foley was noted for his sacred material. Throughout his long and distinguished career, Foley recorded with the Browns Ferry Four, Ernest Tubb and Kitty Wells. Among his hits

were 'Smoke On The Water', 'Tennessee Saturday Night', 'Chatanooga Shoeshine Boy', 'Just A Closer Walk With Thee' and 'Hearts Of Stone'. He was also the composer of 'Old Shep'.

TENNESSEE ERNIE FORD: Born Fordtown, Tennessee, in 1919. Though Ford became eventually noted for his religious albums, his contributions to country music were considerable over the years. He also played an important role in the development of country music on radio and TV, having appeared on WOPI, Bristol, Tennessee (1937), WATL, Atlanta, Georgia (1939), WNOX, Knoxville, Tennessee (1941), KFXM, San Bernardino, California (1945) and many others. Ford was the first western type entertainer to play the London Palladium. His many hits include 'Mule Train', 'Anticipation Blues', 'Smokey Mountain Boogie', 'Sixteen Tons', 'The Ballad Of Davy Crockett' and 'Hick Town'.

LEFTY FRIZZELL: Born in Corsicana, Texas, Lefty's influence on modern country music was not recognized for many years. The

originator of 'laid back' singing, Frizzell first came to prominence in 1950 when he wrote and recorded the uptempo honky tonk song 'If You've Got The Money I've Got The Time' for the Columbia label. He followed that initial success with a string of hits, including 'Always Late', 'Mom and Dad's Waltz', 'I'm An Old, Old Man' and 'Forever'. For the next seven years his popularity went into a decline and it wasn't until 1959 when he recorded the definitive version of 'Long Black Veil' that he returned to popularity, albeit fleetingly. The record became a country classic and though during the '60s Frizzell recorded three more hits, 'Saginaw, Michigan', 'James River' and ''Gator Hollow', his success was short-lived. Frizzell died in 1975 from a heart attack.

BOBBIE GENTRY: Born in Chickasaw County, Mississippi, Bobbie wrote and recorded the award-winning 'Ode To Billie Joe' in 1967 and subsequently cut a number of other hits, some with Glen Campbell.

DON GIBSON: One of the most prolific composers of the last generation, Gibson contributed countless best-selling songs to the country catalogue. Many of his songs were covered by pop artists, including Ray Charles and Roy Orbison, and a number of

them were based on everyday sayings and personal experiences. His best works were 'Oh Lonesome Me', 'Blue, Blue Day', 'Too Soon', 'Give Myself A Party', 'I Can't Stop Loving You' and 'A Legend In My Time'.

LLOYD GREEN: Alabama-born Green was sometimes called America's finest steel guitarist. A professional musician from the age of ten, Green rose to become one of Nashville's most highly innovative and acclaimed session men. Over the years, his steel guitar and dobro were heard on records by Henry Mancini, Peter, Paul and Mary, Charley Pride, Ann-Margret, Crystal Gayle, Warner Mack, Johnny Paycheck, Lynn Anderson and Don Williams. In 1966, Green stepped out as a solo artist and recorded several steel guitar albums for the now defunct Little Darlin' label. He was an integral part of the Nashville 'sound', along with Charley McCoy and Johnny Gimble.

JACK GREENE: Born Maryville, Texas, in January, 1930. A former drummer-vocalist with Ernest Tubb's Texas Troubadours, Greene's recording career began with 'The Last Letter', a track on a Tubb album. The song was so successful that Tubb urged his drummer to leave the band and try for a solo career. Greene did eventually leave the Troubadours and in 1967 his first single, 'All The Time', recorded for Decca, made the national country charts. Four subsequent singles became big hits and in 1967 his version of Dallas Frazier's 'There Goes My Everything' was voted Song Of The Year by the Country Music Association. Along with

his band, the Jolly Giants, and co-vocalist Jeannie Seely, Greene was one of the most successful live performers in American country music.

MERLE HAGGARD: Haggard was a genuine Okie and was born in Oklahoma in 1937. He was already well established in country music when he wrote and recorded two patriotic songs, 'Okie From Muskogee' and 'The Fighting Side Of Me', both of which endeared him to America's hippy set. With various terms of imprisonment for theft behind him — including a spell in San Quentin — Haggard epitomized the 'bad boy made good' syndrome so popular in the US.

Haggard's boyhood country music idols were Jimmie Rodgers, Lefty Frizzell and Bob Wills, and their respective styles influenced his music to a large degree. While in prison, Haggard discovered a talent for writing lyrics and many of the songs he later recorded were his own. Over the years he composed such standards as 'Sing Me Back Home', 'Daddy Frank (The Guitar Man)', 'Branded Man', 'Silver Wings', 'Today I Started Loving You Again', 'Irma Jackson' and 'It's All In The Movies'. He recorded for Capitol and had over 30 albums to his credit, including tributes to Jimmie Rodgers and Bob Wills.

TOM T. HALL: An outstanding songwriting talent with numerous country hits to his credit but best-known for 'Harper

Valley PTA', recorded by Jeannie C. Riley in 1968. Hall was a Kentuckian and based the majority of his songs on personal observations. Fronted a backup band known as the Storytellers and also composed 'Country Is', 'The Year Clayton Delaney Died', 'Ballad Of Forty Dollars' and 'Salute To A Switchblade'.

HAWKSHAW HAWKINS: Hawkins didn't live long enough to make a marked impression on country music through several of his singles figured prominently in the charts over the years. His most notable songs were 'Soldier's Joy', 'Slow Poke', 'Sunny Side Of The Mountain' and 'Rattlesnakin' Daddy'. Hawkins's style was earthy and basic, but 'Lonesome 7-7203', released on the King label in 1963, pointed to a possible new direction for him. He lost his life in a plane crash, alongside Patsy Cline and 'Cowboy' Copas.

JOHNNY HORTON: Horton made a minor impact during the rockabilly era with 'Honky Tonk Hardwood Floor' but really came into his own with a series of 'historical' ballads, beginning with 'The Battle Of New Orleans' and followed by 'Springtime In Alaska', 'Johnny Reb', 'North To Alaska', 'Sal's Got A Sugar Lip' and 'Sink The Bismarck'. Horton scored in the British charts on two occasions. He was born in Tyler, Texas, in 1929 and died in an auto wreck in 1960. Known as 'The Singing Fisherman', Horton recorded for Dot, Mercury and Columbia and was a popular guest on the *Louisiana Hayride* radio show.

DAVID HOUSTON: A descendant of both Sam Houston and Robert E. Lee, Houston enjoyed a successful if largely unspectacular recording career, beginning with 'Mountain Of Love' in 1963.

In 1966 he won two Grammy awards for his recording of 'Almost Persuaded'. He recorded for Epic and was an accomplished yodeller.

FERLIN HUSKY: Born Hickory Grove, Missouri, in 1927. A former DJ working at Bakersfield, California, Husky first made an impact with 'Dear John Letter', a duet with Jean Shepard. He recorded under two other names, Terry Preston and Simon Crum, the latter being a comedy alter ego. Under his Crum pseudonym Husky recorded such hits as 'Morgan Poisoned The Water Hole',

'She's The Wife Of A Country Music Fiddler' and 'Country Music Is Here To Stay'. In his own right Husky was extremely successful with 'Wings Of A Dove', 'Sweet Misery' and 'You Pushed Me Too Far'.

STONEWALL JACKSON: A direct descendant of Andrew Jackson, during his early Columbia Records days Stonewall recorded a number of 'historical' ballads in the style of Johnny Horton. In 1959 he made the British hit parade with 'Waterloo' but was unable to emulate that initial success with subsequent releases. After 1958, when 'Life To Go' was first issued in the US, Jackson was a consistent best-seller with hits like 'Igmoo', 'Leona', 'A Wound Time Can't Erase', 'Old Showboat' and 'Never More Quoth The Raven'. He wrote the country standard 'Don't Be Angry' and hailed from Tabor City, North Carolina.

WANDA JACKSON: Born Maud, Oklahoma, in 1937, Wanda was one of country music's great stalwarts who also enjoyed much popularity as a rock & roll singer. Her successes in that idiom were 'Let's Have A Party' and 'Fujiyama Mama' and although she, like so many other long-established country artists, turned to gospel music, Wanda continued to include the early hits in her stage act. Her greatest country hits spanned the '50s and '60s and her most popular songs from that era were 'In The

Middle Of A Heartache', 'Right Or Wrong' and 'My Baby Walked Right Out On Me'. Wanda was also an accomplished yodeller.

SONNY JAMES: Known as 'The Southern Gentleman', James played fiddle and guitar, and attained international status in 1957 when his version of 'Young Love' entered the British charts. After he first scored, with 'For Rent' in 1956, the rough edges were honed down and James became an established purveyor of

'sophisticated' modern country. In addition to consistent success in the country charts he is also remembered for his production work on Marie Osmond's 'Paper Roses'. As his stage title implies, James was from the south, having been born in Hackeburg, Alabama, in 1929.

JOHNNY AND JACK: Johnny Wright and Jack Anglin and the Tennessee Mountain Boys were among the top performers from 1953 until 1958, scoring in the charts with 'Crying Heart Blues',

'Poison Love', 'Lonely Island Pearl' and 'Stop The World'. Wright was born in Wilson County, Tennessee, in 1914 and was married to Kitty Wells. Anglin was born in Columbia, Tennessee, in 1917 and died in a car crash in 1963 while on the way to the funeral of Patsy Cline, 'Cowboy' Copas and Hawkshaw Hawkins. Wright became a successful solo artist and a member of the Kitty Wells Show.

GEORGE JONES: Jones's first hit was 'Why, Baby, Why' in 1955 and since those days of nasal hillbilly singing and raucous bar-room fiddles, Jones became a living legend. At one stage in

his career he was over-recorded and suffered from a surfeit of product, but from 1972, under the production guidance of Columbia's Billy Sherrill, his releases were carefully regulated. It is interesting to note that Jones once recorded a rocking version of 'Heartbreak Hotel' under the name of Thumper Jones.

By the end of the '50s George was tagged 'the new Hank Williams' and went so far as to earn the title 'Crown Prince of Country Music'. For several years, particularly those involving his association with producer Pappy Daily, Jones's career slumped, but, after his contract with Epic Records was signed, he developed into one of the giants of the country recording industry. His hits include 'Eskimo Pie', 'Poor Chinee', 'She Thinks I Still Care' and 'The Grand Tour'. Jones had numerous joint hits with his wife, Tammy Wynette.

GRANDPA JONES: Born in 1913 in Henderson, Kentucky, Jones was one of the last of the old time banjo pickers in country music and from 1947 was a popular member of the Grand Ole Opry cast. Though his numerous records rarely attained chart status, he became widely known for items like 'Old Rattler', 'Old Rattler's Pup', 'Tragic Romance', 'Eight More Miles To Louisville' and 'Mountain Dew'. He worked with the Browns Ferry Four and Merle Travis. A severe heart attack forced him into semi-retirement but he later made infrequent personal appearances.

DOUG KERSHAW: Born Tiel Ridge, Louisiana, and the writer of over 19,000 songs, the most popular being 'Louisiana Man' and 'Cajun Joe'.

BRADLEY KINCAID: A favourite with North American audiences, Kincaid was one of the few performers to survive the Depression years. Born in Kentucky and known as 'The Kentucky Mountain Boy', he was the first to bring traditional Kentucky songs to radio audiences. Among the successful songs he recorded were 'Sweet Betsy From Pike', 'In The Little Shirt My Mother Made For Me' and 'The Letter Edged In Black'.

CLAUDE KING: Born 1933 in Shreveport, Louisiana. With a vocal style similar to that of Johnny Horton, King reached the forefront at the beginning of the '60s when 'historical' ballads were in vogue. As the result of such hits as 'Big River, Big Man', 'The Commancheros', 'The Burning Of Atlanta', 'Sheepskin Valley' and the classic, 'Wolverton Mountain', King became one of the most successful stars of that period. Unfortunately his popularity began to wane at the turn of the '70s and he is only basically remembered for 'Wolverton Mountain'.

DICKIE LEE: Lee graduated from rock & roll to country. He enjoyed two major pop hits, 'Patches' and 'I Saw The Light', before emerging as a strong country chart artist. Originally, Lee was produced by Jack Clement but his recording career later came under the astute and creative guidance of Allan Reynolds. Lee's most notable country hits included 'Ashes Of Love' and 'Sparkling Brown Eyes'.

WILMA LEE and STONEY COOPER: A popular Virginia-born gospel duo fronting the Clinch Mountain Clan. In 1950, Harvard University voted the Coopers the 'most authentic mountain singing group in America'. The late '50s and early '60s were their most productive years when they were constantly in the country charts with songs like 'There's A Big Wheel', 'Legend Of The Dogwood Tree', 'Big Midnight Special', 'Sunny Side Of The Mountain' and 'Rachel's Guitar'. They became Grand Ole Opry members in 1957.

JERRY LEE LEWIS: Born Ferriday, Louisiana, in 1935, and cut some classic rockabilly sides for the Memphis-based Sun label before veering off into straight rock & roll. Adverse publicity centering around his marriage to a 13 year old almost destroyed the singer's career, but he re-emerged in later years as a fully-fledged country performer. Lewis's hits, which spanned three

styles of music, include 'High School Confidential', 'Great Balls Of Fire', 'Whole Lotta Shakin' Goin' On', 'What Made Milwaukee Famous' and 'To Make Love Sweeter For You'. He retained the pounding piano style that identified his earlier recordings and contributed equally to pop and country.

HANK LOCKLIN: Popular with Irish-American audiences throughout the world, Florida-born Locklin enjoyed great success

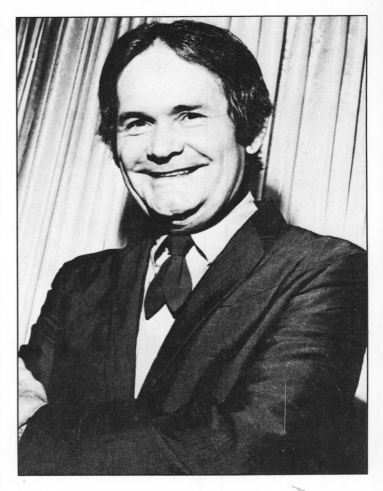

with 'Geisha Girl', 'Send Me The Pillow That You Dream On', 'This Song Is Just For You' and 'Please Help Me I'm Falling', all for RCA.

JOHN D. LOUDERMILK: Born Durham, North Carolina. Primarily a songwriter whose material often crossed over into the pop field. Best known for 'Blue Train', 'The Great Snowman', 'Sad Movies', 'Norman', 'James, Hold The Ladder Steady',

'Abilene', 'Lament Of The Cherokee Reservation Indian', 'Language Of Love', 'Angela Jones' and 'Tobacco Road'.

LOUVIN BROTHERS: The impeccable close-harmony vocalizing of Ira and Charlie Louvin brought them wide recognition throughout the '50s. Like the Blue Sky Boys, the Louvin's work was orientated towards traditional and sacred country music and some of their best records were grouped together under two album headings, 'The Family Who Prays' and 'Satan Is Real'. Charlie was born in 1927 in Henegar, Alabama, and sang lead and played guitar. Ira, born three years earlier, died in a car crash in 1965 shortly after signing a solo contract with Capitol. He played mandolin and provided the tenor harmony.

LORETTA LYNN:
Loretta was among America's top three female country performers for a number of years and her durability could be directly attributed to her prowess as a song-

writer. In 1962 Loretta began writing and recording hits for Decca and her successes include 'Blue Kentucky Girl', 'Fist City', 'Your Squaw Is On The Warpath' and 'Coal Miner's Daughter'. She also recorded a number of hit duets with Ernest Tubb and Conway Twitty.

CHARLIE McCOY:
Nashville's most famous sideman, McCoy was a multi-instrumentalist but his success centered around the harmonica. Associated with Area Code 615 and Barefoot Jerry, McCoy also made the charts in his own right and was forced,

somewhat reluctantly, to cut back on his heavy session schedules to take in personal appearances. Charlie recorded for the Epic label and among his successes were 'Today I Started Loving You Again' and 'Orange Blossom Special'.

SAM AND KIRK McGEE:
Among the first Grand Ole Opry members to actually record in the mid-'20s, and Sam was possibly the first of the Opry cast to play an electric guitar on the show. Though the brothers stayed with the Opry until the '70s, Sam was better known to country enthusiasts for his work with Uncle Dave Macon. Sam, who was born in Franklin, Tennessee, in 1894, was killed in August, 1975, when his tractor overturned.

JIM AND JESSIE McREYNOLDS:
Born in 1927 and 1929 respectively, Jim and Jesse were from Coeburn, in the heart of the Virginia coal fields, and led a popular Bluegrass band known as the Virginia Boys. The group's recording career was less than successful and only one single, 'Diesel On My Tail', recorded for Epic in 1967, became a national hit. The brothers appeared to be unsure of their musical directions on record and it was their live performances that found most favour with country audiences. Over the years, Jesse developed a distinctive cross-picking style on the mandolin. Vocally the brothers were heavily influenced by the Louvin Brothers.

FRANKIE MILLER:
In 1960, Miller was voted Most Promising New Country Artist by American disc jockeys following his highly successful Starday single, 'Black Land Farmer', one of the most strikingly original recordings of the period. Miller began his professional career as a western dance band leader in his home state of Texas. Military service in Korea curtailed his musical

activities for a time and it wasn't until 1959 that he emerged with 'Black Land Farmer'. Several other hits gave Miller international acclaim and he was heralded as the 'new Hank Williams'. He disappeared from the recording scene — and country music — after a brief span of three years, was forgotten and in 1971 was working in a Texas gas station. His few recordings, including 'Prison Grey', 'Tornado' and 'Baby Rocked Her Dolly' became highly-prized collectors' items.

RONNIE MILSAP:
Milsap was born blind and much of his childhood was spent in state schools for the handicapped. He was taught classical music at school and later played rock because ''it was the thing to do''. A native of the Smokey Mountains of Tennessee, Milsap always wanted to play and sing country and,

in order to fulfill his ambition, ultimately moved to Nashville where he landed a residency at Roger Miller's King Of The Road motel. In January, 1973, Milsap cut his first records for RCA and two best-selling singles — 'I Hate You' and 'The Girl That Waits On Tables' — resulted. Within two years Milsap was voted Top Male Vocalist by the Country Music Association.

PATSY MONTANA: First girl western singer to sell a million records — 'I Wanna Be A Cowboy's Sweetheart' on ARC in 1935 — and the first country artist to make a nationwide broadcast. Patsy was born Ruby Blevins in Hot Springs, Arkansas, in 1914.

MELBA MONTGOMERY: After many years as a reasonably successful recording artist, during which time she recorded duets with George Jones ('We Must Have Been Out Of Our Minds') and Charlie Louvin ('Something To Brag About') among others, she

signed to Elektra under the production guidance of Pete Drake. She began to find her true direction and became one of Nashville's lasting stars.

MOON MULLICAN: 'King Of The Hillbilly Piano Players'. Born Polk County, Texas, in 1909 and died in 1967. Became popular for his blues and country repertoire and is remembered for 'I'll Sail My Ship Alone' and 'Sweeter Than The Flowers'.

ANNE MURRAY: Born in Nova Scotia, Anne was not strictly a country artist, but her rendition of Gene McClellan's 'Snowbird'

was a top seller in both pop and country charts in 1970. Later, Anne scored country-wise with 'She Thinks I Still Care'.

WILLIE NELSON: One of Nashville's 'rebel' breed and a great comrade of Waylon Jennings. Nelson was a particularly gifted lyricist and contributed greatly to the country repertoire with 'Funny How Time Slips Away', 'Good Hearted Woman' (with Waylon Jennings), 'The Words Don't Fit The Picture' and 'Shotgun Willie'. For many years Nelson was largely ignored by country music enthusiasts who were slow to accept his rather unique 'jazz-style' vocalizing, but the boundaries of country expanded during the early·'70s and innovative artists of Nelson's calibre

gained fuller acceptance. Originally from Texas, Nelson was popular from the time of his first hit, 'Touch Me', for Liberty Records in 1962.

MICKEY NEWBURY: As a performer Newbury was too sophisticated for wholesale country consumption, but his countless songs were widely covered by Nashville's mainstream

singers. Best works include 'Funny, Forgotten Familiar Feelings' (a hit for Engelbert Humperdinck) and 'American Trilogy' (recorded by Elvis Presley).

NITTY GRITTY DIRT BAND: Jimmie Fadden, Jeff Hanna, Jim Ibbotson, John McEuen and Les Thompson. Formerly a basic rock band featuring one or two country items, the Dirt Band turned to the roots of rural American music in 1971 and recorded a triple LP entitled 'Will The Circle Be Unbroken' — considered by many to be the definitive country album of all time. On this historic album the band were augmented by such names as Jimmy Martin, Doc Watson, Roy Acuff, Bashful Brother Oswald, Merle Travis, Vassar Clements, Mother Maybelle Carter and Earl Scruggs.

THE OSBORNE BROTHERS: Bob and Sonny Osborne, from Hyden, Kentucky, were among the first to realize the potential behind commercialized Bluegrass music and were also among the first 'grass artists to augment the traditional string band sounds with steel guitar, drums and piano. Popular for such songs as 'The Black Sheep Returned To The Fold', 'Ruby Are You Mad', 'She's No Angel' and 'Give This Message To Your Heart'.

TOMMY OVERSTREET: After 1969 Overstreet, from Oklahoma City, enjoyed a fair number of pop-country hits, including 'Heaven Is My Woman's Love' and 'If You're Looking For A Fool'. Tommy was a distant relative of Gene Austin, a popular '30s singing star.

BUCK OWENS: Born August 12, 1929, in Sherman, Texas. Owens created one of the most distinctive modern country music sounds of the '60s by injecting multi-tracked vocals and a hard-driving, twangy lead guitar into his recordings. The Owens sound borrowed much from the western swing bands who had reigned supreme from the late '20s until the beginning of the '50s. Originally a guitarist, Owens built the sound of his band (the Buckaroos) around his own distinctive style. The majority of songs

recorded by Owens during his halcyon days were of his own creation and a goodly proportion became standards. Among the most popular songs recorded by this influential artist are 'Tiger By The Tail', 'My Heart Skips A Beat', 'Crying Time', 'Wham Bam', 'Heartbreak Mountain' and 'Maybe If I Close My Eyes'. Another of Owen's notable achievements was to establish Bakersfield, California, as a country music recording centre.

VERNON OXFORD: Born June 8, 1941, in Benton County, Arkansas. Ironically, Oxford was better known in Britain than in

the States, where he was considered to be 'too country'. Oxford originally signed with RCA in 1965 but, following one or two single releases, was dropped by the company. He later enjoyed a cult following in the UK and his fans were influential enough to encourage RCA's British office to release an album in 1973. Sales of this particular album led to Oxford being re-signed to RCA Victor the following year. No hits, as such, but popular for: 'Watermelon Time In Georgia', 'How High Does The Cotton Grow', 'Mama', 'The Old Folks Home', 'Field Of Flowers' and 'Giving The Pill'.

OZARK MOUNTAIN DAREDEVILS: Comprised John Dillon (guitar, vocals, autoharp, piano and dulcimer), Steve Cash (harp, vocals and poetry), Randle Chowning (guitar, vocals, harp and mandolin), Michael Granda (bass and vocals), Larry Lee (drums,

guitar, piano and vocals) and Buddy Brayfield (piano), this oddly-named group fused together country, rock & roll and elements of traditional Appalachian music to form their own individual sound. The group's first album was recorded in England at Olympic Studios.

GRAM PARSONS: Following his death in October, 1973, from a drug overdose. Parsons was heralded as one of the most creative of all country-rock performers. Parsons's father, Coondog Connors, was a local country artist and the family lived in Waycross, Georgia. During his teens, Gram became involved with Barry Tashien and they formed a group called Barry and the Remains, which ultimately became the International Submarine

Band. After one rather abortive album for LHI Records, Parsons joined the Byrds and his interest in country music greatly influenced the group's musical directions. Parsons later left the Byrds and, together with Chris Hillman, formed the legendary Flying Burrito Brothers. When the Burritos' music began to veer away from Parsons's original concept, he left the group and virtually drifted into obscurity, finally re-emerging in 1973 to record his first solo album, 'GP', an acknowledged masterpiece containing many basic country roots. Following Parsons's tragic death that same year, Warner Brothers released a second solo album, 'Grievous Angel', featuring Emmylou Harris and Linda Ronstadt. There is little doubt that Parsons did much to enhance the popularity of modern country music, but only after his death was his genius recognized.

DOLLY PARTON: Dolly was undoubtedly America's leading female country vocalist, though first achieving chart success as late as 1967 with 'Dumb Blonde', for the Monument label. Only when she signed with RCA and eventually joined the Porter Wagoner Show did her true talents as a songwriter emerge, however. Born in the Tennessee mountains in 1946, Dolly frequently wove folksy themes into her songs. Among her most successful compositions were 'Tennessee Mountain Home', 'Joshua', 'Old Black Kettle', 'In The Good Old Days (When Times Were Bad)', 'J. J. Sneed', 'Love Is Like A Butterfly', 'The Seeker' and 'We Used To'. During her association with Porter Wagoner, Dolly enjoyed a number of vocal duet chart successes with such songs as 'Last Thing On My Mind', 'Daddy Was An Old Time Preacher Man', 'Tomorrow's Forever', '(Just) Someone I Used To Know' and 'We'll Get Ahead Someday'.

JOHNNY PAYCHECK: Paycheck made a minor impact in the days of rockabilly as Donny Young, but it wasn't until his association with Nashville's Billy Sherrill that his career really began to flourish. A previous association with Little Darlin' Records produced six substantial country hits for Paycheck, including 'Lovin' Machine' and 'Don't Monkey With Another Monkey's

Monkey'. At one time Paycheck was virtually on skid row and it became widely reported that he "had a drinking problem". Determination, coupled with Sherrill's brilliance as a creative producer, however, finally established Paycheck and he became among the top attractions on the American country music circuit.

JIMMY PAYNE: Missouri-born Jimmy Payne is of special interest in view of his popularity in the UK. In Nashville, Jimmy was known primarily as a songwriter, with the multi-million-selling 'Woman, Woman' to his credit, but following an initial British tour in 1974, his popularity grew in the UK and many people believed he would emulate the success of George Hamilton IV.

MINNIE PEARL: Sarah Ophelia Colley Cannon was born in Centerville, Tennessee, in 1912 and early in her career created one of America's most lovable country characters, Minnie Pearl, from Grinder's Switch. Minnie Pearl was primarily a comedienne but also recorded a number of successful singles, including 'How To Catch A Man' and 'Giddy-Up Go (Answer)'. She was also a member of the Grand Ole Opry. Elected to the Country Music Hall of Fame in 1975.

CARL PERKINS: Known in the mid-'70s as 'the man behind Johnny Cash', Perkins enjoyed diverse success in both rock & roll and country fields. One of the original performers on the legendary Sun roster, Perkins laid down some of the early rock & roll classics before re-emerging as a country performer. He became an integral part of the Johnny Cash Show. Among Perkins's widely-acclaimed hits are 'Blue Suede Shoes', 'Matchbox' and 'Country Boy's Dream'. Perkins also wrote such hits as 'Daddy Sang Bass' and 'Blue Suede Shoes'.

STU PHILLIPS: Phillips was one of the few non-Americans to be accepted by American country music audiences. Born in Canada, he worked in radio production and later sung with the Edmonton Light Opera Company. He became very successful in Canada with such self-penned items as 'The Champlain & St. Lawrence Line', 'The Eskimo Song' and 'Star Child'. Phillips later moved to Nashville and recorded half-a-dozen hit singles for RCA and was, at one time, tipped to replace the late Jim Reeves. In later years, however, Phillips met with little success on record, although he still commanded a large fan following.

THE PHIPPS FAMILY: Probably the most successful and authentic of all Carter Family 'copyists', this stalwart musical family led by A. L. Phipps did much to preserve the sounds and songs of the acclaimed Carters. Although the recordings of the Phipps Family rarely sold in quantity, over the years the Family enjoyed a small but loyal following at various American folk and country music festivals, including Newport.

WEBB PIERCE: During the early '50s, Pierce recorded some of country music's acknowledged classics, including 'Back Street Affair', 'That Heart Belongs To Me' and 'Wondering'. When rock & roll became the new craze, Pierce was one of the few country artists to adapt successfully and his recordings in the rockabilly

idiom became minor classics. When the rock & roll fever levelled off and country music began to re-emerge, Pierce was able to maintain his popularity and during the '60s he made the charts with 'Fallen Angel', 'Sands Of Gold' and 'Saturday Night' among others. His most popular all-time recordings were 'Tupelo County Jail', 'In The Jailhouse Now' and 'I Ain't Never'.

RAY PRICE: Price, originally known as 'The Cherokee Cowboy', was one of country's most consistent hit makers and between 1952 and 1975 his name was rarely out of the country charts. Among his earlier successes were 'Don't Let The Stars Get In Your Eyes', 'Release Me' and 'Crazy Arms', but he later scored heavily in pop and country fields with 'She Wears My Ring', 'For The Good Times' and 'I Won't Mention It Again'. He joined the cast of the Grand Ole Opry in 1952.

CHARLEY PRIDE: Several Negro performers achieved moderate success in the country music field, including DeFord Bailey (probably the first), Stoney Edwards and O. B. McClinton, but Mississippi-born Charley Pride was the first to take the world by storm. When Pride's first RCA singles began to make an impact

at the end of the '50s. Prior to that Rainwater had enjoyed a considerable country following as the result of hits like 'Gonna Find Me A Bluebird' and 'Get Off The Stool'. He was born in Wichita, Kansas, in 1925 and originally intended to be a veterinary surgeon.

JERRY REED: One of Nashville's most accomplished guitar pickers, Reed also wrote under his real name of Hubbard and was perhaps best-known outside the US for 'A Thing Called Love', recorded by Johnny Cash. Reed was also a master of the comedy recitation and achieved great success with 'Amos Moses', 'Lord, Mr. Ford' and 'Tupelo Mississippi Flash'. He also appeared in the movie *W. W. And The Dixie Dancekings*.

JEANNIE C. RILEY: The 1972 edition of the *Country Music Who's Who* credited Jeannie with eight country hits, including 'Harper Valley PTA'. Following her international success with this most famous of all Tom T. Hall songs, Jeannie received a

on the charts, his management were careful not to let it be known that he was coloured. Such problems were ultimately resolved, however, and he became one of the giant superstars of Nashville. His numerous hits include 'Does My Ring Hurt Your Finger', 'The Snakes Crawl At Night', 'Is Anybody Goin' To San Antone', 'Amazing Love' and 'Hope You're Feelin' Me'.

JOHN PRINE: Prine was something of a hybrid performer whose material appeared equally acceptable to folk, country and

pop audiences, and his most notable composition was 'Paradise', recorded by the Everly Brothers and the Country Gentlemen, among others.

MARVIN RAINWATER: A part-Cherokee Indian, Rainwater first came to the attention of pop fans with his raucous rock hit 'Whole Lotta Woman' and equally infectious 'Dance Me Daddy'

Grammy for the Best Female Country Vocal in 1968. Jeannie's other hit recordings include 'The Rib' and 'Oh, Singer', but none matched the appeal of 'Harper Valley PTA' and she later enjoyed only limited success.

MARTY ROBBINS: Born near Glendale, Arizona, in 1925, Robbins's long career took in an interesting array of musical styles, including pop, Hawaiian, western and country. His early Columbia 'Gunfighter' collections were later considered to be classics and it is for this type of material that he is best remembered. In spite of his associations with the American west, Robbins achieved

notable success with such songs as 'A White Sports Coat And A Pink Carnation', 'Don't Worry', 'Singing The Blues', 'El Paso', 'Devil Woman', 'The Hanging Tree' and 'My Woman, My Woman, My Wife'. He also appeared in three western movies *Buffalo Guns, The Gun And The Gavel* and *The Badge Of Marshall Brennan*.

CARSON J ROBISON: Known as 'The Kansas Jayhawk', Robison was among the most prolific of all country songwriters during the '20s and '30s. Born in Kansas in 1890, Robison recorded for numerous labels, including Conqueror, Oriole, Romeo, Supertone, MGM and RCA. His most popular composition was 'Life Gets Tee-jus, Don't It' but he also wrote 'Naomi Wise', 'Wreck Of The Number Nine', 'Left My Gal In The Mountains' and 'Down In The Little Green Valley'. In 1924 he formed an association with Vernon Dalhart and played guitar on the latter's million-selling 'Wreck of the Southern Old '97'. Robison died in 1957 leaving behind a vast legacy of authentic-sounding songs and ballads, most of which remained to be exploited fully.

JOHNNY RODRIGUEZ: Sounding like a combination of Merle Haggard and Lefty Frizzell, Rodriguez was a consistent hit-maker from his debut in 1972 with 'Pass Me By'. Born in Sabinal,

Texas, 90 miles from the Mexican border, Rodriguez was originally dubbed 'the singer with the Tex-Mex sound' resulting from his habit of featuring Spanish and English lyrics in his songs.

LINDA RONSTADT: Born in Tucson, Arizona, in 1946, Linda Ronstadt first came to the attention of pop fans via a relatively short-lived three-piece group called the Stone Poneys. After

playing in and around Los Angeles during the middle half of the '60s, the group finally secured a recording contract with Capitol, resulting in several impressionable, if not best-selling discs and were best remembered for their hit 'Different Drum'. In 1968 the group broke up and Linda became a solo artist with a strong leaning towards country music. Although she later scored a number of chart successes, Linda Ronstadt was perhaps best known as a backing singer for artists like Hoyt Axton.

JOHNNY RUSSELL: A prolific writer and successful recording artist, Russell's song 'Act Naturally' was a hit for Buck Owens and the Beatles. He later scored heavily with 'Red Necks, White Socks And Blue Ribbon Beer'. Russell recorded for RCA.

EARL SCRUGGS: Born Cleveland County, North Carolina, in 1924, Scruggs was the first to introduce the three-finger style five string banjo to Bluegrass in 1945. Many historians credit Scruggs with actually inventing the method, but it is an acknowledged fact that musicians like Snuffy Jenkins and Smith Hammed had been experimenting with a similar picking technique

considerably earlier. Scruggs was a member of Bill Monroe's Bluegrass Boys when he introduced the revolutionary three-finger style and it changed the whole structure of the Bluegrass genre. Scruggs left Monroe in 1948 and with Lester Flatt formed the Foggy Mountain Boys.

BILLY JOE SHAVER: Shaver was a member of Nashville's 'new breed' of country songwriters and whilst not fully accepted as a performer with stone-country audiences, his material was widely covered by the likes of Tompall Glaser, Johnny Cash, Tom T. Hall and Waylon Jennings. Among the most popular of Shaver's songs were 'Old Five And Dimers Like Me', 'Willie The Wandering Gypsy And Me', 'Slow Rollin' Low', 'Ride Me Down Easy', 'Honky Tonk Heroes' and 'Jesus Was Our Saviour And Cotton Was Our King'.

JEAN SHEPARD: Another of country's acknowledged all-time greats, Jean's most successful period spanned the '50s when she recorded 'Dear John Letter', 'Forgive Me John' (both with Ferlin Husky), 'Beautiful Lies', 'Satisfied Mind' and 'Second

Fiddle'. Born in Paul's Valley, Oklahoma, Jean attended Visalia High School in California. In 1959 *Cash Box* magazine voted her Top Female Country Singer.

SHEL SILVERSTEIN: *Playboy* cartoonist Silverstein enjoyed recognition as a composer for some years and among the artists he wrote for were Dr. Hook and the Medicine Show, Bobby Bare, Johnny Cash, Barbi Benton and Tompall Glaser. Silverstein's seemingly endless list of hit songs includes 'A Boy Named Sue', 'Musical Chairs', 'Take The Singer With The Song', 'Hills Of Shiloh', 'Sitting In The Kitchen' and 'Marie Laveau'.

CAL SMITH: Born in Sallisaw, Oklahoma, on April 7, 1932. Formerly a 'stooge' for Todd Mason, a trick rider and rope expert, Cal eventually broke into the nightclub scene and sang with Kitty Dibble and Her Dude Ranch Wranglers. In 1954, Smith became a

regular on a television series, *California Hayride*. Eventually Cal secured a place in Ernest Tubb's band, the Texas Troubadours. He left the group in 1968 and embarked on a highly successful solo career, brought to a peak in 1974 when his record 'Country Bumpkin' was voted Single Of The Year by the Country Music Association.

CARL SMITH: Born in Maynardsville, Tennessee, in 1927, Smith was one of the most successful stars of the '50s and had sales of over 15,000,000 records to his credit. Among his most successful singles, many of them classics, were 'If Teardrops Were Pennies', 'Let Ole Mother Nature Have Her Way', 'Trademark', 'Ten Thousand Drums', 'Loose Talk', 'Deep Water' and 'Faded Love And Winter Roses'. Smith joined the Grand Ole Opry in 1950. He was married to former country star Goldie Hill.

CONNIE SMITH: Popular RCA and CBS hit maker discovered by Bill Anderson. Connie's first major country hit was 'Once A Day' recorded in 1964. Other successes included 'Cincinnati, Ohio' and 'Where Is My Castle'. Connie was one of a growing band of country artists who devoted much of their non-playing time to Christianity.

HANK SNOW: Clarence Eugene Snow was born in Nova Scotia in 1914 and his recording career spanned over 40 years. Hank gained much of his initial inspiration from the singing of Jimmie Rodgers and, following a period of fairly limited success in Canada, finally moved to America. Snow called himself the 'Singing Ranger' and built up a substantial following in Canada

and America via such recordings as 'The Prisoned Cowboy' and 'Brand On My Heart', but it wasn't until 1950, when he recorded 'I'm Movin' On' that he attained true stardom. This song remained in the *Billboard* country charts for 49 consecutive weeks and Snow remained a consistent hit maker. Like his former idol, Jimmie Rodgers, Snow identified with the railroad for much of his career and many of his initial hits were associated with locomotives, including 'Big Wheels', 'The Golden Rocket' and 'The Last Ride'.

JOE SOUTH: Singer/songwriter notable for 'Games People Play', 'Don't It Make You Wanna Go Home' and 'Rose Garden'.

RED SOVINE: Born Charleston, West Virginia, in 1918, Woodrow Sovine enjoyed a long and successful career in country music. Much of his entertainment experience was gained on such radio stations as WCHS, Charleston, West Virginia; KWKH *Louisiana Hayride*, Shreveport, Louisiana, and WSM *Grand Ole Opry*, Nashville, Tennessee. Sovine's hits include 'Little Rosa', 'Giddyup Go', 'I Didn't Jump The Fence', 'Phantom 309' and 'I Know You're Married But I Love You Still'. His 1956 recording of 'Why, Baby Why' (a duet with Webb Pierce) became one of country's classics.

BILLIE JO SPEARS: Former Capitol recording artist who became an international country star as the result of 'Blanket On The Ground'. While with Capitol, Billie Jo scored heavily with six hit recordings between 1969 and 1971, before moving to the United Artists label.

STATLER BROTHERS: Originally a close-harmony gospel group, the Statler Brothers were 'discovered' by Johnny Cash. As a gospel group they were known as the Kingsmen and the name change came when Cash decided that they would fit into his travelling show. Only two of the Statlers were actually brothers – Don and Harold Reid – and they took their name from a box of tissues! The other members of the quartet were Lew DeWitt and Phil Balsley. In 1965, the group recorded 'Flowers On The Wall', which became an international best-seller, and later scored heavily with 'Bed Of Roses', 'Ruthless', 'That'll Be The Day' and 'Whatever Happened To Randolph Scott?'.

RAY STEVENS: While not looked upon as a thoroughbred country boy, Stevens nevertheless utilized many of Nashville's country sounds in his pop recordings, the most successful of these being 'Gitarzan', 'Everything Is Beautiful', 'Bridget The Midget', 'The Streak' and 'Misty'.

WYNN STEWART: Born Morrisville, Missouri, in 1934. Although Stewart enjoyed sporadic hits from 1960, when he took 'Wishful Thinkin'' into the nation's country charts, until the early '70s, like so many other innovative performers, his talents passed by virtually un-noticed. In the same mould as Lefty Frizzell, Stewart was a superb vocal stylist and a gifted song-writer and was among the originators of contemporary up-tempo country sounds.

THE STONEMAN FAMILY: Ernest V. 'Pop' Stoneman was the founder-member of this large and highly entertaining musical family. Ernest was among the earliest of country performers to achieve wide success, and his version of 'Sinking

Of The Titanic' became a million-seller in the '20s. Pop Stoneman sired no less than 23 children and among those to be associated with the Stoneman Family were Roni, Pattie, Donna, Van, Jim and Scotty.

CARL STORY: Story was a former truck driver who turned to the field of gospel music and became one of its most revered exponents. With his group, the Rambling Mountaineers, Story recorded such gospel favourites as 'I Heard My Mother Weeping', 'Paul And Silas' and 'Old Gospel Ship'.

STRINGBEAN: Dubbed 'The Kentucky Wonder', Dave 'String-bean' Akeman was born in Annville, Kentucky, in 1915 and, though virtually unable to read or write, became a banjo virtuoso. Akeman came by his unusual nickname when an announcer on station WLAP in Lexington, Kentucky, forgot his name. Akeman was playing banjo with Cy Rogers and the Lone-

some Pine Fiddlers at the time and when the band was due to go on the air for one of their regular programmes, the announcer, looking at Akeman's 6 feet 2 inch-tall figure, simply forgot his name and called out: "Come on out and play for us, stringbean." Stringbean played the banjo in the style of the old banjo pickers like Uncle Dave Macon, and enjoyed a large following among college audiences. On November 10, 1973, Stringbean was murdered in his Center Hill Lake, Nashville, home. He is remembered for songs like 'Mountain Dew', 'Moonshine In Them Old Kentucky Hills', 'Suicide Blues' and 'Barn Yard Banjo Picking'.

HANK THOMPSON: With over 100 chart entries to his credit Hank Thompson was an undisputed stalwart and with his group, the Brazos Valley Boys, sold in excess of 30 million records after 1948. Thompson's popularity began during the western swing era and he was one of the few artists to survive the decline of this highly individual style of Texas country music. Hits included: 'Humpty Dumpty Heart', 'Green Light', 'Squaws Along The Yukon', 'Whoa Sailor', 'Waiting In The Lobby Of Your Heart', 'Smokey The Bar' and 'Honky Tonk Girl'. Originally known as

'Hank The Hired Hand', Thompson was a graduate of Princeton University, New Jersey.

MEL TILLIS:
A long-standing favourite with American audiences, Tillis was the writer of 'Detroit City' and countless other songs. Other notable country hits included 'Commercial Affection', 'Goodbye Wheeling' and 'Arms Of A Fool'. Appeared with Burt Reynolds in the movie *W. W. And The Dixie Dancekings.*

TOMPALL and the GLASER BROTHERS:
Tompall, Jim and Chuck Glaser were among the world's top vocal groups and their close-harmony singing was among the finest ever recorded. Though the three brothers were equally talented, Tompall was undoubtedly the driving force behind the trio and their hits included 'Gone On The Other Hand', 'Through The Eyes Of Love', 'The Moods Of Mary', 'Wicked California' and 'Gone Girl'. Their voices can be heard on many early recordings by Johnny Cash and Marty Robbins. The Glaser Brothers eventually went their separate ways in country music and each achieved individual success. Of the three, Tompall was probably the best-known, mainly for his work with Waylon Jennings.

MERLE TRAVIS:
Born in Rosewood, Kentucky, in 1917, Travis was one of the most innovative and respected of all country guitarists. He was also a noteworthy composer with songs like 'Sixteen Tons', 'No Vacancy', 'Smoke, Smoke, Smoke' and 'Dark

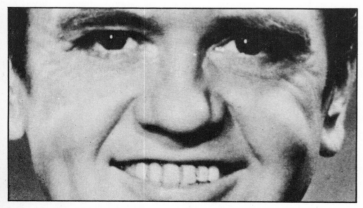

As A Dungeon' to his credit. He made an impressive movie debut in *From Here to Eternity.*

ERNEST TUBB:
Known as 'The Texas Troubadour', Tubb was born in Ellis County, Texas, in 1914 and was a true musical legend. Together with his famous western band, the Texas Troubadours, Tubb began recording hits in 1944. Originally greatly influenced by Jimmie Rodgers, Tubb was, in turn, an influential musical force. His long-running radio show, *Ernest Tubb's Midnight Jamboree*, was beamed out to as many as 300 different stations. Broadcast from his Nashville record shop, Ernest's programme was popular with visiting artists. A prolific composer, Tubb's best-known song is the oft-recorded 'Walking The Floor Over You'. Among his other hits were 'Soldier's Last Letter', 'Try Me One More Time', 'Slippin' Around', 'Waltz Across Texas', 'Too Old To Cut The Mustard', 'Goodnight Irene' (with Red Foley) and 'Sweet Thing'.

TANYA TUCKER:
Tanya was a mere 14 years old when she became a singing sensation and, while still a teenager, became one of country music's hottest properties. Possessing a richly mature voice, Tanya became famous for songs containing provocative lyrics, including 'What's Your Mama's Name', 'Blood Red And Goin' Down', 'The South's Gonna Rise Again'

and 'Old Dan Tucker's Daughter'. Tanya first signed with the Columbia label and her earlier hits were produced by Billy Sherrill. A move to MCA Records brought about a gradual change of style aimed at marketing her as a middle-of-the-road artist. Tanya's later hits included 'Lizzie And The Rainman' and 'San Antonio Stroll'.

PORTER WAGONER:
Born West Plains, Missouri, in 1927. Former clerk and butcher. Played guitar and gained early entertainment experience via local radio stations, before signing with the Grand Ole Opry in 1957. Porter's numerous singles and albums for RCA were seldom out of the country charts and he was famous for 'Company's Coming', 'The Carroll County Accident', 'The Cold Hard Facts Of Life', 'Cold Dark Waters Below', 'Skid Row Joe', 'Green, Green Grass Of Home' and 'What Would You Do?' His association with Dolly Parton led to an impressive number of hit recordings, among them being 'We'll Get Ahead Someday', 'Last Thing On My Mind' and 'Just Someone I Used To Know'. Wagoner fronted a popular country band known as the Wagonmasters and hosted a syndicated television series, *The Porter Wagoner Show.*

DOC WATSON: Watson was born blind in Deep Gap, a mountainous area separating the states of Tennessee and North Carolina. Doc's father, General Watson, taught him to play the fiddle and banjo, and from the same family source Doc learned a wealth of early ballads and sacred melodies. Two years after he enrolled at the Raleigh School for the Blind, he began to excel on guitar. It was for his guitar playing that Watson was widely known and both folk, jazz and country music audiences regarded him as among the very best in his field. During his early years he absorbed the music of Riley Puckett, Gid Tanner and the Carter Family, and his wide repertoire was full of songs from what many term the Golden Age of Country Music — the '20s and '30s.

KITTY WELLS: Born Muriel Deason in Nashville, Tennessee, on August 30, 1919, Kitty was yet another country legend. In 1954 Governor Frank Clement bestowed the Most Outstanding Tennessee Citizen Award upon her and five years later she signed a life-time contract with Decca Records. Known during the '50s and '60s as the 'Queen of Country Music' Kitty's contributions to country music were immesurable. From 1952 until

1968, she recorded 57 hit singles, including 'It Wasn't God Who Made Honky Tonk Angels', 'Making Believe', 'Dust On The Bible', 'Amigo's Guitar' and 'She's No Angel'. Several of her hits were duets with such top-ranking artists as Webb Pierce and Red Foley. When her hits began to trail off, Kitty relinquished her contract and signed with Capricorn, where she enjoyed a second round of success. Kitty was married to Johnny Wright, one-time partner of the late Jack Anglin.

DOTTIE WEST: Born October 11, 1932, in McMinnville, Tennessee. Formerly married to steel guitarist Bill West. Originally a crinoline-clad country girl, Dottie later emerged as one of

Nashville's most sophisticated performers. Her recording career began with Starday Records but became truly established after she signed with RCA. Dottie's many hits included 'Here Comes My Baby', 'Love Is No Excuse' (a duet with the late Jim Reeves), 'Reno', 'Country Girl', 'Rings Of Gold' (with Don Gibson), 'Forever Yours' and 'Country Sunshine'. The latter hit was one of Dottie's biggest, originally being a Coke commercial.

SLIM WHITMAN: In 1955, Slim Whitman's recording of 'Rose Marie' remained at the top of the British charts for 12 weeks, one of the longest-standing No. 1 singles in Britain, and over a period of 8 weeks the record sold 650,000 copies. Other big-selling singles that helped to consolidate Whitman's phenomenal following in the UK included 'Indian Love Call' and 'Secret Love'. Whitman's record sales fluctuated in America and he made the charts on an average of once or twice every two or three years. In Britain, however, he continued to command a huge fan following, and in 1974 his single 'Happy Anniversary' was placed high in the pop charts. During his 1974 UK tour, Whitman played to approximately 250,000 people, outselling most major pop tours.

THE WILBURN BROTHERS: Teddy and Doyle began their entertainment careers picking and singing on the streets of Thayer, Missouri, but eventually progressed to Decca and the Grand Ole Opry. Though they later stopped recording, the

Wilburn Brothers were prolific hit makers throughout the '50s and '60s, and among the songs associated with them are 'Go Away With Me', 'Hey Mr. Blue Bird', 'Trouble's Back In Town', 'Roll Muddy River' and 'I'm Gonna Tie One On Tonight'.

DOC WILLIAMS: Doc and his travelling country music show were among the last of the old tent performers once so popular in the rural areas of America. Doc performed largely in the old-time idiom and was famous for such songs as 'Willie Roy The Crippled Boy', 'Broken Memories', 'My House Of Broken Dreams' and 'Snowdeer'. Williams was a veteran artist who, while seldom attaining national chart status, nevertheless enjoyed a loyal following throughout West Virginia, New Hampshire, Maine and Vermont. He was an exceptional guitarist and the first country performer to publish a guitar tutor.

DON WILLIAMS: Williams began to emerge in his own right in the mid-'70s following a successful period as a member of the oddly-named Pozo Seco Singers. He was a prolific writer with songs like 'Oh Misery', 'Down The Road I Go', 'Your Sweet Love', 'The Shelter Of Your Eyes', and 'Too Late To Turn Back Now' to his credit. A number of chart successes, including some best-selling albums, ensured Williams of a bright future.

Williams managed to create a distinctive instrumental and vocal sound of his own and was one of the most refreshing new talents to emerge since the early '60s. With dobro taking the lead on many of his songs, backed up by banjo, Jew's-harp, fiddles and pedal steel guitar, Williams, together with his innovative

producer Allan Reynolds, put a little of the roots back into country music. Among his hits were 'You're My Best Friend' and '(Turn Out The Light And) Love Me Tonight'.

HANK WILLIAMS JNR.:
After striving to succeed in the country music business while retaining his father's illustrious name, Hank Williams Jnr. eventually evolved his own identity and

after 1964 recorded a long list of hit singles and a number of popular albums. He was best known for 'Custody', 'Cajun Baby' and 'Removing The Shadow'. In 1975 Williams sustained severe head and facial injuries when he fell down 500 feet of rock during a hunting trip.

MAC WISEMAN:
Wiseman was one of the most outstanding bluegrass vocalists of all time and had long associations with Earl Scruggs, Bill Monroe and Lester Flatt. Mac was born in Crimora, Virginia, in 1925, and worked on such shows as the WSB *Atlanta Barn Dance, The Louisiana Hayride*, the WRVA *Old Dominion Barn Dance* and the *Grand Ole Opry*. The *Country Music Who's Who* credited Mac with just two hit recordings, 'Jimmy Brown The Newsboy' and 'Johnny's Cash and Charlie's Pride', but during his long and distinguished career, he was associated

with innumerable other successful recordings, among them 'I'll Still Write Your Name In The Sand', 'The Ballad Of Davy Crockett', 'Goin' Like Wild Fire' and 'I Wonder How The Old Folks Are At Home'. For a number of years Wiseman was A & R manager for Dot Records, for whom he recorded.

SHEB WOOLEY:
Outside country music circles Wooley was probably best remembered for his role as Pete Nolan in the long-running television series *Rawhide* and a brief but impressive appearance in the classic movie *High Noon*. Musically, Wooley

made an impact on an international scale with a novelty rock & roll hit, 'The Purple People Eater'. A gifted comedian, Wooley created the character Ben Colder and under that name enjoyed numerous hits based on popular country songs.

FARON YOUNG:
Born Shreveport, Louisiana, in 1932, Young was one of several country entertainers to venture successfully into movies. Though only associated with low-budget westerns, Young earned some acclaim for his roles in *Hidden Guns, Raiders of Old California* and *Daniel Boone*. Young was one of the first regulars on the influential *Louisiana Hayride* and his appearances on the highly-rated show resulted in his teaming up with Webb Pierce for a road show. At the beginning of the '50s, Young signed with Capitol Records and quickly made the charts with 'Tattle Tale Tears'. He followed this initial hit with over 20 other successful singles for the label before changing to the Mercury roster, where he continued to produce hits. In 1972 Young's recording of 'Four In The Morning' entered the British charts and remained there for a period of 20 weeks. Other hits recorded by Young include 'Live Fast, Love Hard And Die Young', 'All Right', 'If You Ain't Lovin'', 'That's The Way I Feel', 'Riverboat', 'Country Girl', 'The Yellow Bandana' and 'Step Aside'. Young was also co-owner of *Music City News*, one of America's most successful country music journals.